THE STEP-BY-STEP GUIDE TO

DESIGNING & STYLING YOUR HOME

BY NATASHA ROCCA DEVINE

theinteriorsnrd.com

Designed by Anne Moloney
Edited by Shari Last
Published by Orla Kelly Publishing
Printed by KPS Colour Print

Orla Kelly Publishing
27 Kilbrody,
Mount Oval,
Rochestown,
Cork
Ireland

KPS Colour Print,
Knock,
Co Mayo
F12PF66
Ireland

TO DAVID, FREYA, MONTE, MY FAMILY,
FRIENDS & EVERYONE WHO HAS SHOWN
ME SUPPORT... INCLUDING YOU

GRAZIE MILLE

Natasha xxx

CONTENTS

Theme: Art Deco | Gatsby
Project: Robswall by Hollybrook
Client: Hollybrook Homes
Agent: Knight Frank Ireland
Photographer: Declan Cassidy

INTRODUCTION

The Interiors NRD Studio offers bespoke interior design and project management services to residential and commercial clients in Ireland and internationally online. The studio's founder, Natasha Rocca Devine, has experience working and studying in Los Angeles, Boston, London, Ireland and across Europe. Natasha's portfolio includes award-winning showhome design and style consultation in Ireland and London, where Natasha studied interior design.

As a member of the Interiors Association of Ireland, Natasha recently designed showhomes for Foxburrow and Hollybrook Homes. She was a guest speaker at Ideal Homes 2021 and 2022, as well as the designer of the Ideal Homes Stage for DFS. She also wrote for the 'Home Help' panel of *The Sunday Times*. In May 2021, Natasha launched the 'Secret Garden' candle second scent, as part of a limited-edition sustainable candle collection with leading Irish brand La Bougie. In every project, Natasha incorporates sustainability, eco design and Irish design as core features.

Since opening in 2018, The Interiors NRD Studio has received more than 23 awards for a portfolio of projects. Most notably, clients include Knight Frank and Hollybrook Homes developers. Natasha's work for agent Owen Reilly included filming for RTE One's *Find Me A Home* TV show.

Using her skills as a journalist, Natasha takes time to write and share her interiors knowledge online. While she continues guest speaking and presenting radio items, she also contributes to magazines and newspapers including *The Sunday Business Post*, *The Sunday Independent* and *The Times*.

Natasha gained her first Masters in Journalism and Media Communications at Griffith College, Dublin, followed by a second in Interior Design and Architecture at KLC School of Design, London. Since early on, Natasha has taken a keen interest in philanthropy, working with former Vice President Al Gore's Climate Reality Project and supporting mental health, animal rights, homeless support and children's charities.

THE INTERIORS NRD STUDIO

The Interiors NRD Studio was created by Natasha Rocca Devine and offers bespoke interior design and project management services to residential and commercial clients in Ireland and internationally online. The studio was created from Natasha's experience working and studying in Los Angeles, Boston, London, Ireland and across Europe. Natasha's portfolio includes award-winning showhome design and style consultation in Ireland and London, where Natasha studied interior design.

Photographer: Barry McCall
Location: The Wilder Townhouse
Stylist: Catherine O'Connell
Make Up: Zoe Clarke
Hair: GS Treschic

I LOOK FORWARD TO HELPING YOU CREATE THE HOME OF YOUR DREAMS TO EITHER LIVE IN, SELL OR RENT

LET'S GET STARTED....

LOTS OF LIGHT,

Natasha xxx

WHAT IS YOUR DESIGN PROJECT?

ARE YOU DESIGNING A SPACE FOR YOU TO LIVE IN?

YES ——————— NO

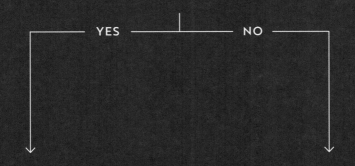

DO YOU OWN
THE SPACE?

ARE YOU DESIGNING
FOR SHORT-TERM?

YES   NO   YES   NO

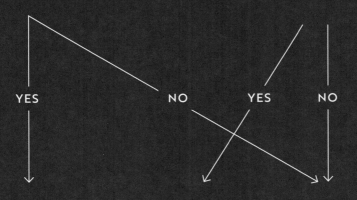

1   2   3

INTERIOR
DESIGN

INTERIOR
STAGING

INTERIOR
STYLING

INTERIOR
DESIGN

*I AM GOING TO MAKE
EVERYTHING AROUND ME
BEAUTIFUL — THAT WILL
BE MY LIFE.*

ELSIE DE WOLFE

WHAT IS
INTERIOR DESIGN?

Interior design is a fully integrated design service of a house, apartment or specified space. It should reflect the style and functionality required by the residents or occupants, while ensuring that it is both functionally and aesthetically pleasing.

NRD DESIGN TIP

Before commencing your design project, request quotes from at least three certified contractors to work out the average cost and maintain your budget. For every contractor, ensure to get contracts, in writing, signed to include project dates, agreed costs and the terms and conditions for any changes to the contract.

Theme: Oceanic Luxury
Project: Robswall by Hollybrook
Client: Hollybrook Homes
Agent: Knight Frank Ireland

Theme: Giorno e Notte
Project: Robswall by Hollybrook
Client: Hollybrook Homes
Agent: Knight Frank Ireland
Photographer: Declan Cassidy

Theme: Classic Contemporary
Project: Mount Stewart
Client: Hollybrook Homes
Agent: Hume Auctioneers
Photographer: Declan Cassidy

YOUR DESIGN
QUESTIONNAIRE

These are key questions to ask yourself before you begin designing. Realistic plans will save you time, money and stress in the future. Now it's question time!

1

Describe your current home. What do you like about it? What is missing? What do you not like? Why do you want to change the space you have?

....
....
....
....

2

What is your lifestyle? Do you live alone or with a family? Are you at home often? Do you work at home? Will this be a long-term home for a family or a short-term home for tenants?

....
....
....
....

3 How much time and energy are you willing to invest to maintain your home interiors project? Will you live on site or will you move to a rental or other location?

....

....

....

....

4 If you are thinking of extending specific spaces, what functions or activities will the new spaces need to accommodate?

....

....

....

....

5 Have you hired an interior designer? Or a painter, electrician or other contractors?

....

....

....

....

6 What do you think the extension/renovation/new home should look like? (E.g. contemporary classic, vintage, modern)

....

....

....

....

7

How much can you afford to spend on this design project?

....
....
....
....
....

8

How soon would you like to commence? When are you hoping to be settled into your new home or extension? Are there rigid time constraints?

....
....
....
....
....

9

Do you have strong ideas about design? What are your design preferences? How would you describe your style? Will you have an overall or room-by-room theme?

....
....
....
....
....

10   Which brands do you like or dislike? Are you thinking of getting new furniture? Have you thought about whether it would be vintage, upcycled, or of a bespoke design?

....

....

....

....

....

11   Is there anyone in the family with a disability, or any other factors whereby mobility problems may need to be addressed?

....

....

....

....

....

12   Would you like to consider additional options that could help optimise your building's performance towards zero energy inputs, healthy materials, or other sustainability goals? Have you researched relevant grants, products or materials to do so?

....

....

....

....

....

YOUR *DIY* STARTER KIT

1. Paint Brush Set
2. Paint Roller
3. Masking Tape
4. Silicone Gun
5. Work Gloves
6. Scraper
7. Wrench
8. Hammer
9. Drill
10. Saw
11. Measuring Tape
12. Sandpaper
13. Spirit Level
14. Screwdrivers
15. Cutters

YOUR INTERIOR DESIGN **TO-DO LIST**

TASK	✓

YOUR INTERIOR DESIGN **TO-DO LIST**

TASK	✓

YOUR INTERIOR DESIGN **NOTES**

YOUR INTERIOR DESIGN **NOTES**

INTERIOR
STAGING

*THE DESIGNER'S JOB IS
TO IMAGINE THE WORLD,
NOT HOW IT IS, BUT HOW
IT SHOULD BE.*

TERENCE CONRAN

WHAT IS
INTERIOR STAGING?

Staging is specialised interior design, styling a home, apartment or commercial space pre-sale or pre-rental to increase the sale/rental price, while assisting the pace of the sale or rental.

A 'showhome' is designed as an aspirational interior design project that should appeal to potential buyers or clients, while maximising the square footage of each space.

NRD STAGING TIP

Are you staging to sell or rent? Or both? Focus your project on your three USPs (Unique Selling Points). These are unique to this property and will be the reason the buyer or rental client will be enticed to visit, and hopefully purchase or the rent, the property.

Theme: Art Deco | Gatsby
Project: Robswall by Hollybrook
Client: Hollybrook Homes
Agent: Knight Frank Ireland
Photographer: Declan Cassidy

STAGING *TO SELL*

Apartment living area before staging

Apartment living area after staging

Project: RTE - *Find Me A Home*
Agent: Owen Reilly Estate Agents

Penthouse before staging

Penthouse after staging

Project: 20 Hanover Riverside
Agent: Owen Reilly Estate Agents

STAGING *TO RENT*

Client: Burrow Holiday Park
Photographer: Philip Lauterbach
Sponsor: DFS

WHAT ARE THE
TOP 10 TIPS?

Whether you are preparing your home or an investment property for sale, rental or listing on Airbnb, apply these tips to help you get the maximum price and best response from buyers or clients.

IMAGINE THE CLIENT

Decide who the optimum client is and stage the space based on their lifestyle, needs and your budget. Plan the staging around your ideal client and put in some of your own style if it would suit the clientele.

CHOOSE THE USP'S
(UNIQUE SELLING POINTS)

Decide what the key USPs of the space are and work from there. Keep it simple. For example, if there is a superb view, invest in emphasising the window features. If there is a beautiful garden, invest in additional pieces to accentuate the outdoor space.

SURVEY THE SPACE

Access the floor plans of the space and/or take photographs of each room and outdoor area. Plan for each space by making a contents list and a to-do list. Most importantly, plan out where new and existing furniture can be placed. Then create a list of what is missing to complete the staging.

BUDGET BALANCED

Based on your to-do list, create a budget and use this to research furniture, home accessories and styling. Also, create a list of who and what will be required to help you on each step of this process. This will help build your team, from painters and movers to cleaners and gardeners, and so on.

CLEAR OUT

Remove all idle existing furniture, or move them into a small area in each room so you can plan the best use of the space. Donate unwanted furniture to charity or sell at a local vintage market. This will not only give you more space inside the property, but it will also raise money you can re-invest or give to family, friends or charity – which is a positive way to let go of personal things.

CLEAN UP

Budget for cleaners before and after the project. Think about carpet cleaners and window cleaners too. Air out the space to ensure it is free of smells, such as pets or cooking, and choose scented candles to provide specific smells that reflect the ambience you wish to create.

RE-COLOUR

Invest in a re-paint of the entire space. Alternatively, focus on key areas such as doors and window frames to emphasise nice structural features. Opt for neutral colours such as white, off-white and cream to make the space look larger. Alternatively, choose on-trend colours to highlight certain aspects of the space in a different way. You could even re-spray furniture to restore older pieces if the budget allows.

LIGHT-IT-UP

Open the windows to allow the most natural light into the space. Combine this with layers of lighting to create a space that is bright but not overbearing. Place mirrors in hallways and smaller areas as these can help add depth and give the appearance of a larger space.

MIX & MATCH

When purchasing home accessories and furniture, opt for a mix of new pieces and vintage, which can be re-sprayed or touched up to bring some classic style into your space. Or you could rent furniture from a staging company – or borrow from family and friends – particularly if you require your existing furniture with you as you move during this period.

OUTDOOR LIFE

A garden is a luxury for many apartments, particularly for city homes, so ensure the windows are clean and balcony areas are staged too, with seating areas if there's space. Spray the paving, varnish any wooden furniture and make the most of plants. If the property has a garden, ensure it is well kept. Plant new bulbs if necessary and fix any run-down fencing so it looks its best. This will help you retain the highest sellable or rental value.

STAGING AN *INTERIORS PROJECT*

Apply pai
or wallpap

Add in
accessories

Apply scents

Tablespace

Add in new pendant lighting

Create zones e.g. dining, tv, reading

Create layers in lighting

...eate ...heme

Include sustainable products

Theme: Art Deco | Gatsby
Project: Robswall by Hollybrook
Client: Hollybrook Homes
Agent: Knight Frank Ireland
Photographer: Declan Cassidy

WHAT ARE THE BENEFITS OF *STAGING?*

100%

of estate agents believe that home staging is a helpful marketing tool when having a property listed.

57%

say that they get a return on their investment with home staging.

71%

of estate agents say staging increased viewings.

51%

say staged properties sell twice as fast non staged ones.

Staging a home can increase the offer value on a property by

75%

71%

of estate agents would recommend staging properties from the outset of marketing.

31%

of buyers claimed staging their home increased the offer on their home.

80%

of staged properties go on offer in the first four weeks according to property professionals.

Source: Home Staging Association of UK & Ireland 2020

YOUR STAGING **TO-DO LIST**

TASK	✓

YOUR STAGING **TO-DO LIST**

TASK	✓

YOUR STAGING **NOTES**

YOUR STAGING **NOTES**

3

INTERIOR
STYLING

99

YOU CAN'T USE UP
CREATIVITY.
THE MORE YOU USE,
THE MORE YOU HAVE.

MAYA ANGELOU

WHAT IS
INTERIOR STYLING?

Styling is when a designer clears the existing space and creates an aesthetically pleasing environment, whether for an office block, residential homes or seasonal projects.

NRD STYLING TIP

When styling, set a theme and budget before you start. The theme will be the core focus of each room, and the connecting details are key to the styling success. For a sale or rental, less is more, so remove any idle furniture and accessorise to the overall theme. For personal styling projects, retain your own style. Take risks but always keep it simple.

Theme: Modern Traditions
Project: Foxburrow
Client: Hollybrook Homes
Agents: Hume Auctioneers

Theme: Giorno e Notte
Project: Robswall by Hollybrook
Client: Hollybrook Homes
Agent: Knight Frank Ireland
Photographer: Declan Cassidy

INTERIOR STYLING *TIPS*

Apply these styling tips to help you sell, rent or bring your home to life again! Use these tips with a rental or sales property to add those final details your clients will never forget.

THEME THE SCHEME

Begin your styling project by creating a general mood board on digital platforms such as Instagram or Pinterest, or even using magazine cuttings. You could also create specific mood boards for each room or for different features (e.g. lighting, paint colours, etc). Preparation is key, particularly if you plan to make permanent changes such as painting the walls, wallpapering or installing lighting – because these renovations would be costly and time-consuming to redo if you're not happy with the result.

FIND YOUR FOCUS

Look for your 3 USPs (Unique Selling Points) and invest in them. Keeping the USPs in mind, choose simple styling options. Look at each room and space and ask yourself: 'Does this have a USP or not?' For example:

> If the property boasts a superb view, invest in window features.

> If the property has a magnificent living room, focus your styling there. Accessorise the other rooms, but invest the most in the best room(s) to keep costs minimal.

> If there is a garden, invest in plants and outdoor seating to accentuate the outdoor space.

> If there are spare rooms, style them as a home office/playroom/exercise area and accessorise accordingly.

CLEAR & CLEAN

Remove any unwanted furniture and make sure the space is spotless! Hire cleaning teams or clean as you go to save time and prevent delays at the end.

PAINT & PAPER

Re-paint the entire space if possible, or paint key areas or structural features. Apply wallpaper to feature walls and work to a theme centred around this. For a simple design, opt for neutral colours such as white, off white and cream to help make the space look larger. Alternatively, choose on-trend colours or wallpapers in key rooms to make a statement.

RECYCLE, REUSE, REINVENT

Purchasing furniture is fun and usually a good investment, yet it can be costly and time-consuming, particularly when furnishing entire homes. Think about recycling and re-using some of your existing furniture pieces. For example, wrap your wood furniture. Or re-upholster fabrics. Both can save costs and restore beautiful, aged pieces. You can avoid a costly kitchen renovation by wrapping or respraying the cabinets in a new colour. This will re-invent the space in keeping with your new theme and make it look new and modern.

ALWAYS ADD ART

Art is at the core of all design. Every project space is a 'gallery' to curate. For interiors projects, choosing the right art is fundamental to the project's success. Staging projects depend heavily on art. Getting it right can affect the sale of the home for agents and clients alike. So, find your local gallery, visit art and trade fairs or research online. Every space – from small apartments and unique architectural spaces to large homes over multiple floors – can be greatly enhanced by art. The art, photography or sculpture you add to the space will work to connect each room and create a unified design throughout.

A considered and consistent approach to colour, material and texture is fundamental to styling a home successfully.

SILVER METALLIC TRIMMING

GLASS FOR DINING SURFACES

GREY FABRIC FOR SOFT FURNISHINGS

Theme: Oceanic Luxury
Project: Robswall by Hollybrook
Client: Hollybrook Homes
Agent: Knight Frank Ireland

STYLE YOUR
BEST SHELF

1. Plant Life

2. Mirrors & Frames

3. Glassware

4. Candles & Diffusers

5. Discreet Storage

6. Personal Touches

7. Books, Magazines & Vinyl Records

YOUR STYLING **TO-DO LIST**

TASK	✓

YOUR STYLING **TO-DO LIST**

TASK	✓

YOUR STYLING **NOTES**

YOUR STYLING **NOTES**

PERSONAL
GUIDES

**EVERYTHING YOU CAN
IMAGINE IS REAL.**

PABLO PICASSO

WHAT IS YOUR
DESIGN PERSONALITY?

Take your time and tick one box after each question. Once completed, you will have a better idea of your design personality!

1 WHICH IS YOUR FAVOURITE COLOUR FROM BELOW?

☐ A. Black

☐ B. Green

☐ C. White

☐ D. Navy

2 WHICH IS YOUR FAVOURITE ROOM FROM BELOW?

☐ A. Kitchen

☐ B. Dining Room

☐ C. Living Room

☐ D. Office - Library

3 HOW WOULD YOU DESCRIBE YOUR DREAM HOME?

☐ A. Creative | Colourful

☐ B. Sleek | Serene

☐ C. Relaxing | Chic

☐ D. Open Plan | Efficient

4 WHY ARE YOU DESIGNING YOUR HOME?

☐ A. I want to create a home which will be ideal for having more guests, parties and day-to-day fun in the space

☐ B. I want to bring a sense of past and present into my home to create a sense of purpose

☐ C. I want to create a sense of style which combines both practicality and comfort in each space in my home

☐ D. I want to create a more organised space with precise zones, modern finishes and high-tech utilities

5 HOW DO YOU WISH TO FEEL IN YOUR NEW HOME?

☐ A. I want to bring together all my travel, art and experiences to inspire for myself and anyone who visits

☐ B. I want to have strong themes bringing in history and culture to create a balanced home to work, relax and enjoy the space

☐ C. I want to relax, unwind and detach from the world with my family and friends

☐ D. I want to feel calm in a space that is organised and allows me to maximise each day

6 WHICH WOULD BE YOUR FAVOURITE FINISH?

☐ A. Studs

☐ B. Velvet

☐ C. Fabric

☐ D. Leather

7 WHAT IS YOUR FAVOURITE MUSIC GENRE?

☐ A. Rock 'n' Roll

☐ B. Blues

☐ C. Jazz

☐ D. Classical

8

WHAT WORD WOULD YOU SAY BEST DESCRIBES YOUR FASHION STYLE?

- [ ] A. Eclectic
- [ ] B. Curated
- [ ] C. Timeless
- [ ] D. Refined

9

WHICH WINDOW TREATMENTS WOULD YOU OPT FOR?

- [ ] A. Roman Blinds
- [ ] B. Voile
- [ ] C. Curtains
- [ ] D. Electric Blinds

10

WHAT WORD SPEAKS TO YOU MOST IN TERMS OF DESIGN?

- [ ] A. Sustainable
- [ ] B. Recycled
- [ ] C. Snug
- [ ] D. Economical

UNCOVER YOUR *STYLE*

Check which letter you ticked the most
(or two or three) to see your preferred style(s)!

Project: Robswall by Hollybrook
Client: Hollybrook Homes
Agent: Knight Frank Ireland
Photographer: Declan Cassidy

MOSTLY A'S
RETRO GLAM

You are a Rock 'n' Roll designer, delighting in bringing back the 1960s glam design to take centre stage at home. Each room will be full of colour, patterns, art and accessories, creating an inspiring, eccentric style – a home ideal for guests, parties and pure enjoyment 24/7.

Project: Robswall by Hollybrook
Client: Hollybrook Homes
Agent: Knight Frank Ireland
Photographer: Declan Cassidy

MOSTLY B'S
MID-CENTURY MODERN

You are a mid-century modern muse bringing your innate glam to life. You are someone who enjoys relaxing surrounded by art during the day – and who can host parties as grand as the Great Gatsby at night. You will curate your home with fusion flair, bringing the past and future together.

Project: Mount Stewart
Client: Hollybrook Homes
Agent: Hume Auctioneers
Photographer: Declan Cassidy

MOSTLY C'S
CLASSIC CONTEMPORARY

You are a balanced, calm, cool and collected designer who will bring together a serene space ideal for relaxing and unwinding from a busy lifestyle. Your guests will enjoy this space so much, they may never wish to leave.

Client: Burrow Holiday Park
Photographer: Declan Cassidy

MOSTLY D'S
MODERN STYLE

You are a modern visionary with a home of clean, crisp and crystal-clear lines, fabrics and finishes. Each room will have a functional purpose, including top-of-the-range electronics. There is no doubt you will have the most chic and efficient home in town.

YOUR DESIGN STYLE **NOTES**

YOUR DESIGN STYLE **NOTES**

PROJECT
MANAGEMENT

Every interior design project will require a starting point, a schedule, plans, lists, an understanding of the teams or individuals involved, knowledge of equipment required and a budget, along with a review process and an end point. A project manager will manage the whole process. The project manager might be the designer, depending on the size of the design firm, or someone else – perhaps a contractor, a freelance manager, or even the client themselves.

Project management is an extensive job and someone with specialist skills and experience will be most likely to achieve the intended targets. Particularly with interior design, hiring a project manager can save you up to 20%, so it is a very important role.

As a natural organiser, I thrive when planning for my projects. However, just like life, regardless of how prepared you are, there is no way to predict the changes and challenges that arise during a design project. My aim is to help you avoid these. Preparation is key and here are some guidelines to assist you.

> **NRD PROJECT MANAGEMENT TIP**
>
> To take on this role yourself, you need to have a realistic plan in place, work hard to stay on budget, and remain organised and calm. It is important to be a good communicator, and work on being flexible and adaptable. Make sure this role is for you – otherwise, find the right person to manage the project before you get started. Let's check out the main duties.

- Draft proposals based on client requirements
- Plan, budget and execute projects (including final delivery)
- Coordinate with stakeholders
- Coordinate with contractors
- Conceptualise design
- Estimate projects
- Research products and maintain sample libraries
- Communicate and negotiate with suppliers
- Procure materials and maintain documentation
- Manage schedules
- Guide staff and enforce project deadlines
- Conduct site visits
- Conflict resolution
- Interact with clients, contractors and suppliers
- Keep up-to-date with codes, legal standards and grants
- Remain flexible when projects change
- Follow all planning and building regulations and ensure the applications are processed
- Apply for grants where permissible

THE INTERIOR DESIGN PROJECT MANAGEMENT CYCLE **OFTEN CONTAINS VARIOUS STAGES**

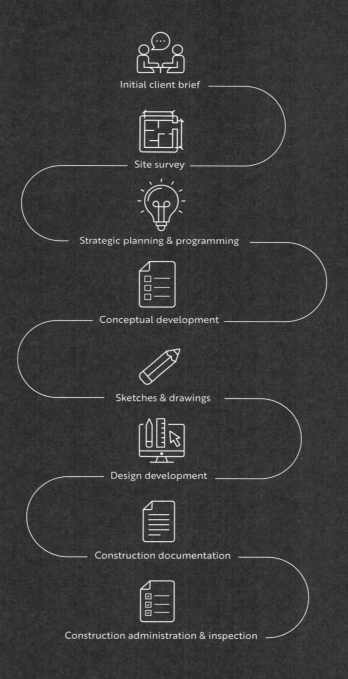

Initial client brief

Site survey

Strategic planning & programming

Conceptual development

Sketches & drawings

Design development

Construction documentation

Construction administration & inspection

YOUR PROJECT MANAGEMENT
TOP 20 CHECKLIST

Let's help you become your own in-house project manager with this checklist:

1 Move off site if possible for health, safety and practical reasons. ☐

2 Invest in interior design project management software. ☐

3 Set a project schedule and communicate timelines for each phase to all involved. ☐

4 Set daily, weekly and monthly goals. ☐

5 Get quotes from various builders and contractors. ☐

6 Hire a builder or individual contractors and ask if you need to apply for planning permission and if you are eligible for any relevant grants. If so, follow all required legal and practical steps to process these applications. ☐

7 Create contracts and have these in place with all contractors. ☐

8   Set realistic budgets and perhaps invest in software to manage this. ☐

9   Ensure you are adept with budgeting and invoicing skills or obtain training. ☐

10   Research and create a list of products, including lighting, paint and furniture and update the budget to include these. ☐

11   Get self-build insurance and ensure your teams have insurance. ☐

12   Communicate and ensure your neighbours on either side are aware of the works. ☐

13   Ensure you have the right building materials and equipment. ☐

14   Ensure you have the products ordered in line with the project deadlines. ☐

15   Delegate your work to contractors, family or friends who can help. ☐

16   Organise your digital files so you have everything in place including photography, plans and invoices. ☐

17   Visit and review the site every day, or as often as you can. ☐

18   Review the project and your goals and adjust the schedule and plans accordingly. ☐

19   Always allow extra time at the end of the project, particularly if you are living on site. ☐

20   Remain flexible and have options in place in case things don't work to plan. Keep focused on the end goal. ☐

YOUR PROJECT MANAGEMENT **PLANNER**

JANUARY

FEBRUARY

MARCH

APRIL

MAY

JUNE

YOUR PROJECT MANAGEMENT **PLANNER**

JULY

AUGUST

SEPTEMBER

OCTOBER

NOVEMBER

DECEMBER

YOUR QUOTE *TRACKER*

DATE: COMPANY:

PRICE: SERVICE:

NOTES:

DATE: COMPANY:

PRICE: SERVICE:

NOTES:

DATE: COMPANY:

PRICE: SERVICE:

NOTES:

YOUR QUOTE *TRACKER*

DATE: _____   COMPANY: _____

PRICE: _____   SERVICE: _____

NOTES: _____

_____

_____

_____

_____

DATE: _____   COMPANY: _____

PRICE: _____   SERVICE: _____

NOTES: _____

_____

_____

_____

_____

DATE: _____   COMPANY: _____

PRICE: _____   SERVICE: _____

NOTES: _____

_____

_____

_____

_____

WHAT ARE
MOOD BOARDS?

Mood boards are physical or digital collages that arrange images, materials, text and other design elements into a format that represents the final design's style.

Mood boards can be used for creating brand designs, product designs, website designs and pretty much any other type of design project. They are the key essence of the project. Let's check out some different options.

NRD STAGING TIP

Decide at the beginning of your project which type of mood boards you will use. (You can use both if you wish!). Mood boards will keep you and your team focused on the core design of the project. For all mood boards – but especially digital boards – communicate to your teams that they may change over time. You want everyone to be aware if any changes occur during the project, so your teams and contractors should always check the most up-to-date version of the mood boards.

WHAT TO INCLUDE ON YOUR MOOD BOARD?
TOP 10 FEATURES

1. Colours. For example, the colour scheme per room or as a whole.

2. Your style. For example, the style of theme you would like.

3. Graphic elements. For example, designs that resonate with your style.

4. Typography. For example, fonts or hand lettering.

5. Your passions. For example, family, friends, yoga, bars, restaurants, reading, art or travel.

6. Your ideal customer or the residents of the property. For example, a family, a single male, multiple tenants.

7. Photography. For example, abstract or specific.

8. Physical items. For example, samples of flooring, curtains, wallpaper or fabrics.

9. Similar homes or furniture. For example, photos of rooms, houses or furniture you aspire to emulate.

10. Anything personal to you. For example, images of family, images of jewellery or photographs.

NOW IT'S TIME TO
CREATE YOUR VISION

Mood boards are in essence the 'vision' or 'mood' of the theme and they will bring your style from concept to completion. They really are the feeling and emotion of the space.

On your boards, you can add colours, fabrics and furniture – or have separate boards for each. These will help you – or anyone else – visualise the look and feel of the project. You can also add music, photography and literature, all of which add depth to the board.

For staging and styling in particular, mood boards are key as they will entice the buyers and renters to view and purchase or lease your home. For personal interiors, mood boards will help you create a dream home for you and your family.

Credit: iStock

PHYSICAL MOOD BOARD

In the industry, mood boards are required for client pitches. Designers start the design process with a mood board, often looking to their favourite brands, photographers, magazines, authors or fashion labels for inspiration. Physical mood boards are powerful because they can appeal to more than just our sense of sight. You can include tactile objects on them, including fabric or wallpaper samples. For a team or family, they are a great collaborative tool, and are easy to use when consulting in person.

Having a single, physical mood board makes it clear as to the direction of the project. It removes any uncertainty about the design ideas, which is ideal when lots of different teams and contractors are involved. Yet physical mood boards are limited to being offline. They are perfect for in-house pitches or collaborating in person, but less so for remote consultation. A photo, or even a live video, of a physical mood board will never do it justice. They are also not so easy to change and update as your ideas and projects grow. They run the risk of getting outdated as the project develops. Furthermore, they can get lost, misplaced or damaged on site.

Credit: iStock

DIGITAL MOOD BOARDS

Although they miss out on the opportunity for tactile features, digital mood boards are a widely available and highly adaptable digital tool. There are many free and easy-to-use platforms for creating a digital mood board these days. Additionally, the internet offers endless inspiration – you can search for images and ideas of any style, artist, or decade, and add them to your mood board. You are also not limited by how artistic you are when it comes to putting a digital mood board together.

The main strength of a digital mood board is that it gives you the ability to constantly update it and share the latest version with your teams. Digital mood boards can be created on various platforms and using various programmes, such as Canva, Google Slides, Pinterest, Milanote, Adobe InDesign and Adobe Spark, many of which allow for live online collaboration. While this is a positive, digital mood boards have to be managed and moderated so that a clear final decision is reached after collaborations.

Digital boards are ideal if the project manager is off site, or if there are multiple teams and contractors in various locations. They are fluid and function as a constant work-in-progress throughout the entire design process, which makes them much more adaptable and more environmentally sustainable than physical mood boards.

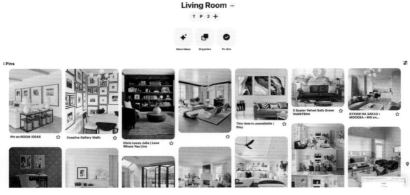

Credit: Pinterest

YOUR MOOD BOARD *PLANNER*

INTERIOR
INSPIRATION

COLOUR

COLOUR

COLOUR

COLOUR

LIGHTING

FLOORING

FABRIC

YOUR MOOD BOARD *PLANNER*

TRAVEL

FASHION

MEDIA

TEXTURES

FINISHES

INTERIOR
INSPIRATION

WHAT ARE
ARCHITECTURAL
PLANS?

Architectural plans are two-dimensional representations that show a proposed development/redevelopment of an area. They include features or elements such as columns, walls, partitions, ceilings, stairs, doors, windows, floors, room designations, door and window call-outs and all details that will be present in the development.

A site plan, or plot plan, is a type of drawing used by architects, landscape architects, urban planners and engineers, which shows existing and proposed conditions for a given area, typically a parcel of land that is to be modified. For buyers or renters, they show the differing options to choose from and the benefits of each.

NRD PLANNING TIP

For interior design, hire an architect or draftsperson to create your plans as they will be the blueprints for your home. I recommend taking a course in SketchUp or working with a specialist on SketchUp or another 3D visual programme. This will help explain your ideas to contractors and they can then work directly off the plans and visuals.

EXAMPLE SITE PLAN

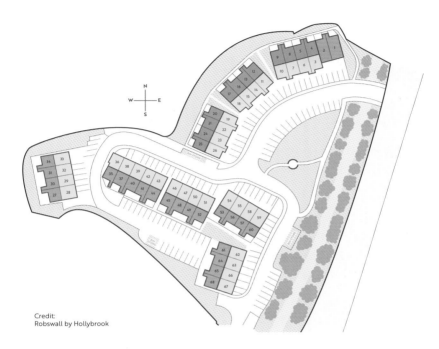

Credit:
Robswall by Hollybrook

A construction plan contains the following elements:

> **Cover Page**: A drawing of the complete project with title, notes and a legend

> **Title Block:** An important section that includes details about the project, site and builders

> **Drawing Scale:** This will help you understand the proportions to which the plan has been drawn

> **Notes:** This section includes specifications, details, information and explanations about the project, design and drawing

> **Legend:** This explains the symbols and abbreviations that have been used in the plan

WHAT ARE
FLOOR PLANS?

Floor plans are architectural drawings that give you a bird's eye view of the space. They show dimension lines, measurements and spatial relationships between objects and fixtures.

Plans provide the builder or designer a physical landscape to look at and serve as the initial blueprint for your design project. As such, they are key to cutting down on money, time and issues throughout the project. Investing in these is crucial to a successful build.

Floor plans are always drawn to scale. The scale will be shown on the map, and usually includes several numbers, such as the dimensions of the room in feet and inches. For example, 1:16 – 3/4 inch = 1 foot, 1:50 – 1/4 inch = 1 foot, 1:100 – 1/8 inch = 1 foot 1:200 – 1/16 inch = 1 foot. There may also be a number that has 'hp' alongside it. This shows the height of the window sill. Numbers alongside stairs will tell you stair height, width and often the number of stairs.

EXAMPLE FLOOR PLAN
TWO-BEDROOM APARTMENT

Credit:
Robswall by Hollybrook

WHAT IS THE PURPOSE OF A *FLOOR PLAN?*

A floor plan is an important document that illustrates what a finished building will look like. Some new homes built by developers hit the market before construction is complete. In such cases, real estate agents use floor plans to provide a sense of a finished house to prospective buyers. All rooms, including the master bedroom, guest bedrooms, dining room, living room, laundry room, master bathroom, and guest bathroom are noted in these house plans, with square footage provided for each room.

Floor plans fit into a larger set of building plans (called either a permit set or a contractor set). These plans include cross-section drawings (or elevations), technical drawings that show construction methods, window and door schedules and a foundation plan. All these documents provide information necessary for the design and execution of the building process, and they are often used to request planning or building permission before the project begins.

EXAMPLE FLOOR PLAN
GROUND FLOOR

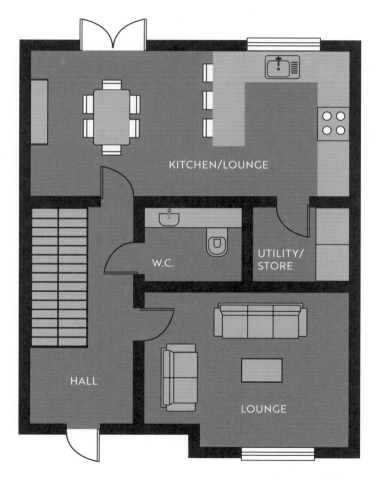

KITCHEN/LOUNGE

W.C.

UTILITY/
STORE

HALL

LOUNGE

FLOOR PLAN
SYMBOLS

To keep things simple, there are universal floor plan symbols to help you understand and visualise the space well. Symbols used in floor plans are standardised so everyone knows what they mean.

WALLS:

Construction drawings will show you both interior and exterior walls. They are shown using a set of parallel solid lines on either side. In most drawings, you will see them as solid lines though sometimes they are depicted with a pattern.

WINDOWS:

A small break in the wall, followed by thin lines along the width, will let you know that there is a window in the space demarcated.

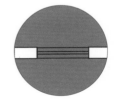

DOORS:

When a door is designated, you will notice a break in the wall. The door will be shown at a right angle to the wall, with a small arc that lets you know which way it swings.

STAIRS:

Stairs are shown as a row of rectangles that may also have the appearance of parallel lines.

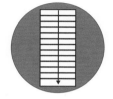

FIXTURES:

Several fixtures may be incorporated into the drawing. Although electrical plans may not be visible, light fixtures will be shown. You can also see fixtures like a sink, shower, bathtub, stove or toilet drawn to an approximation of its actual size. Furniture and other movable fixtures are not usually included in floor plans.

CEILING HEIGHT:

This is not a common element on a floor plan but you may find these dimensions on the plans for the lower floor if the house has multiple levels. It may also be specified in cases where there is an extended ceiling.

KEY ELEMENTS TO
READING A FLOOR PLAN

Compass Mark

Size & Measurement

Walls

Window & Door Placement

Furniture Placement

Stairs

Bedroom, Kitchen & Bathroom

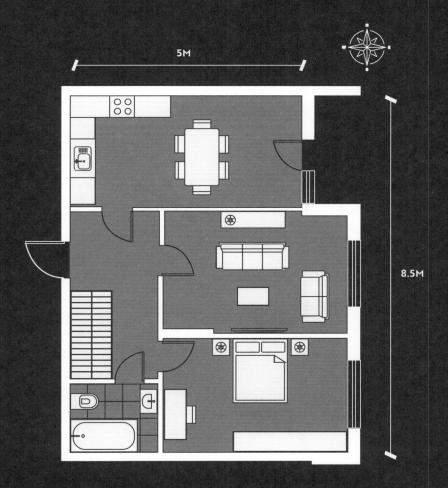

5M

8.5M

AC: Air conditioner   DW: Dishwasher
B: Basin   KIT: Kitchen
CAB: Cabinet   WC: Water closet
CLG: Ceiling   WD: Window
D: Door/dryer   WR: Wardrobe

Credit:
Robswall by Hollybrook

WHAT ARE
ELEVATION PLANS?

An elevation is a vertical face-on image that shows the height, length, width and appearance of a building or structure.

ELEVATION

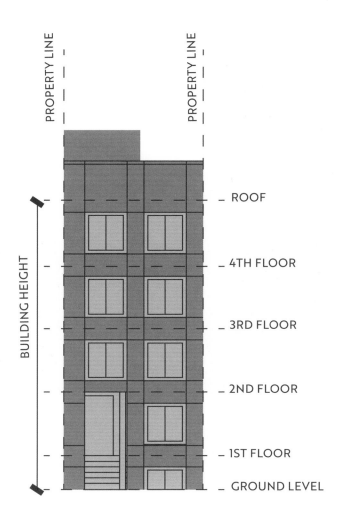

Credit:
Robswall by Hollybrook

WHAT IS A
SECTION?

Section drawings are a specific type of drawing architects use to illustrate a building or portion of a building. It is as if you cut through a space vertically and stand directly in front, looking straight at a cross-section of the building.

SECTION

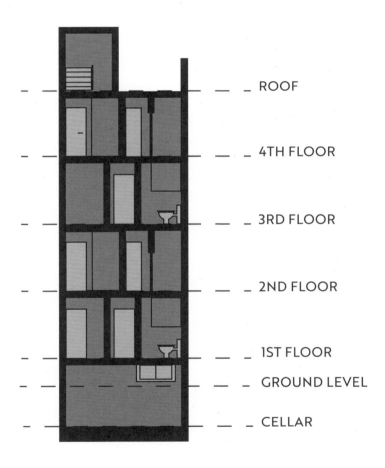

ROOF

4TH FLOOR

3RD FLOOR

2ND FLOOR

1ST FLOOR

GROUND LEVEL

CELLAR

Credit:
Robswall by Hollybrook

SKETCHUP *PLANS*

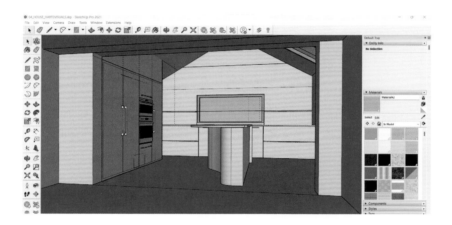

SketchUp 3D Visualisation
Credit: Cillian Harte

3D *PLANS*

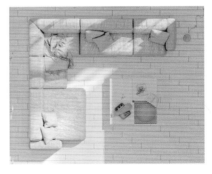

3D Visualisation
Credit: Cillian Harte

YOUR **SKETCHES & PLANS**

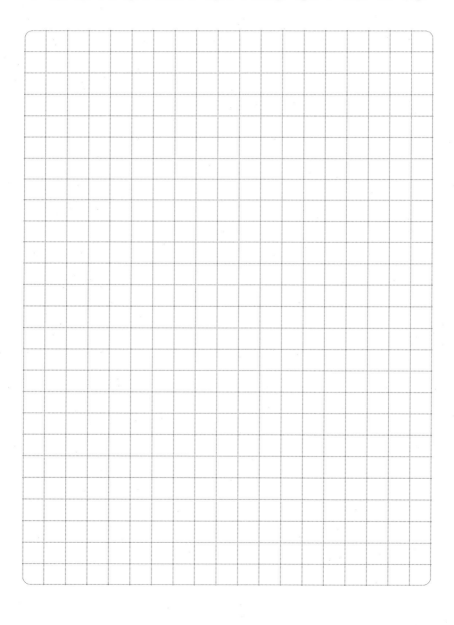

YOUR SKETCHES & PLANS

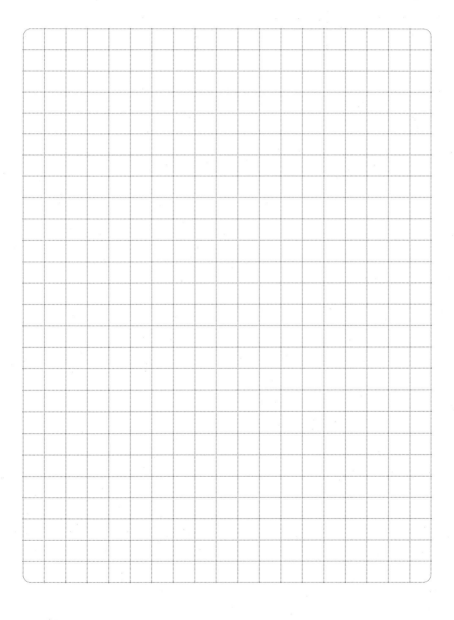

WHAT IS A
COLOUR CHART?

A colour chart is a systematic collection of colours arranged either by the attributes of the colours or their mixing relations. The role of the colour chart is to help keep colour consistent throughout the entire design process.

In interior design, a colour chart or colour reference card is a flat object that has many different colour samples connected together, though they can be viewed separately. These colour charts are available as a single-page chart, or in the form of swatch books or a colour-matching fan, depending on the brand, designer or client preference.

NRD COLOUR TIP

For your own interior design project, create a colour mood and scheme that suits your tastes. For rentals and sales styling, ensure the colour scheme is to your taste but also marketable for clients. Combine with complementary or contrasting wallpaper for the ultimate wow factor!

WHAT IS A
A COLOUR WHEEL?

There are 12 main colours on the colour wheel. In the RGB colour wheel, these are red, orange, yellow, chartreuse green, green, spring green, cyan, azure, blue, violet, magenta and rose.

HUES: Hues are the outer edges on the colour wheel, which are the colours listed above: the primaries, secondaries and tertiaries.

TINT: Adding white to any hue will result in a tint.

TONES: Adding grey (black + white) to a hue will give you a tone.

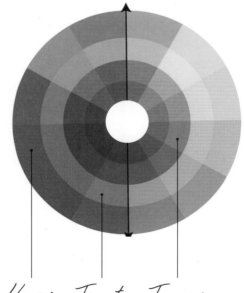

Hues Tint Tones

WHAT ARE THE EFFECTS OF COLOUR *ON INTERIORS & YOUR MOOD?*

The colour of walls and ceilings can dramatically change the atmosphere of a room. Dark colours can make spaces feel small and cosy, while light colours can make rooms feel larger and more open, which is ideal for smaller spaces. The use of colour has a powerful effect on your space, and your mood.

Let's go through the top 10 interiors colours to find your colour mood!

1. WHITE

Background: White is a peaceful hue, frequently used in interior design to reflect light, faith, purity and innocence.

Where To Use: It can be used anywhere in the home. White colours create the sense of a larger space, even when used in a small room. White is associated with cleanliness, so it is ideal for kitchens, bedrooms, halls and bathrooms. White walls, tiles, cabinets and counters look great with textures of dark wood, natural wood and tiles of another colour.

Where Not To Use: If placed in the wrong spaces white can appear dull and sterile. Particularly in larger spaces, white can lack warmth, so ensure to balance it with furniture, soft accessories and other colours.

MEANING

Peaceful

Airy

Innocent

Pure

Youthful

Faith

Freshness

Balance

Silence

2. BLACK

Background: Black is associated with malice and misfortune in various cultures. Fortunately, it also has positive associations, such as formality, elegance and mystery.

Where To Use: Black is often used as an accent colour, in contrast with many other colours. When used carefully, it can be stylish and timeless. Black accents combine well with woods, copper, silver and gold to reflect warmth and splendor, so it is ideal for living rooms, offices and bathrooms.

Where Not To Use: Black does not usually work well as a feature wall because it needs to wrap any room to create a significant impact. It can be complemented with softer colours or accent colours, or you can add touches of black to influence the mood of a room.

MEANING

Modern

Powerful

Sleek

Drama

Mystery

Sophistication

Elegance

Formality

Luxury

Classic

3. GREY

Background: Grey reflects a sense of decorum and most colours are compatible with grey, making it widely popular. It is also mid-way between black and white.

Where To Use: Grey is neutral and is a strong design colour that is easy on the eye. It is a great choice for rooms that require focus and calm, such as dens, bedrooms or offices. Grey complements most other colours.

Grey used alone can be timeless, classic or modern depending on the furniture and finishes, so it is ideal for use throughout the house.

Where Not To Use: Grey used as the primary colour throughout a home might lack in excitement or emotion, so combine it with other colours, either of paint or accessories, for balance.

MEANING
Elegant
Soft
Timeless
Delicate
Refinedw
Calm
Reliable
Professional
Neutral
Mature
Practical
Balance

4. BEIGE

Background: Beige can also be described as cream, taupe, ivory or tan, and it has the superb quality of taking on the characteristics of other colours in a room. Shades of beige are considered stable, traditional, and adaptable and are known to have a calming effect.

Where To Use: Using beige with other colours can bring out your accent colours, thanks to beige's ability to accentuate other colours. It can be used in all rooms throughout the house, ideally in halls, kitchens, bathrooms and bedrooms.

Where Not To Use: If beige is the only colour used, it might appear plain and lacklustre, but it is a great option for a complementary colour.

MEANING
Neutral
Soft
Elegance
Comfort
Simplicity
Relaxation
Warm
Calm
Traditional
Adaptable

5. BLUE

Background: Blue is known to add depth to a space. It is often seen as an indicator of reliability, security and order, and it is also used to provide a zen-like quality and a sense of calm.

Where To Use: Serene blue colours like aqua, turquoise or periwinkle are ideal in a master bedroom, home office, or bathroom. Cool blues can fade out and, as a result, make a room feel larger, so they are ideal for use in smaller spaces. Warm blue shades are best for gathering spaces, including the living room, dining room or kitchen.

Where Not To Use: Dark blue can create a gloomy mood particularly in rooms with no light or sunshine, so avoid using it in small, dark bedrooms or offices.

MEANING
Trust
Spirit
Perspective
Content
Dependability
Determination
Loyalty
Modern
Goals
Serene

6. PURPLE

Background: Purple is an indicator of richness, nobility and health. It also has a relaxing influence, which is often connected to spirituality.

Where To Use: Purple ranges from bright violet to soft lavender so it is best to use the appropriate hue depending on your interiors and personal style. It has a certain theatrical effect, so it is best matched with lighter colours such as soft yellow, pastel pink or white. It is ideal for living rooms, offices and feature walls in bedrooms.

Where Not To Use: Purple can be a very striking colour so it does not always suit kitchens, bathrooms or classic/classic contemporary homes.

MEANING
Creativity
Positive
Fantasy
Dramatic
Wealth
Luxury
Meditative
Stimulation

7. RED

Background: Red is a compelling colour, often known to reflect power, passion and anger – particularly bright reds, which are very visually stimulating.

Where To Use: Shades like ruby and burgundy radiate a warm and welcoming feeling so they are ideal in bedrooms, offices, halls, bathrooms or smaller spaces. Some reds, particularly when amplified by the lighting too, can stimulate appetite, which is why this colour is used in fast-food restaurants around the world.

Where Not To Use: Vivid red is an energising colour, so avoid using it in a bedroom to ensure optimum sleep. Similarly, it fuels appetite, which might not be ideal for a day-to-day dining space.

MEANING

Passionate
Active
Power
Bold
Energy
Youthful
Physical
Excitement
Pioneering
Fearless

8. GREEN

Background: Green is the colour of the earth and reminiscent of nature and outdoors. It is a sign of hope, luck and abundance and it also represents environmental causes.

Where To Use: A cool green can complement a variety of colours. Emerald, mint and lime can all add sophistication to any room in your home. Green looks crisp and clean with white accents. All greens can be stylish and calming when applied in the home.

Where Not To Use: Green is a very strong and bold colour so it is best avoided directly next to other very strong colours, such as blue or red.

MEANING

Balance
Growth
Fresh
Sanctuary
Equilibrum
Positivity
Nature
Generous
Clarity

9. BROWN

Background: Brown is a mixture of the primary colours, red, yellow and blue, so it is known to be an ideal complementary colour. It can make people feel at home and welcomed.

Where To Use: It is an ideal colour for the living room, bedroom, or dining room. It is also associated with nature and can give your interior a rustic feeling, especially when complemented with green. Overall, brown can make you feel secure, grounded and content, so it is ideal for use in bedrooms, living rooms and relaxation rooms.

Where Not To Use: Brown can be a bit dreary if overused in the home, so it is best with complementary colours and other accent colours to maximise its impact.

MEANING
Nature
Relaxation
Structure
Earth
Comfort
Warmth
Stability
Supportive
Reliable
Serious
Wholesome

10. PINK

Background: Pink is an adapted version of red and usually associated with romance or young innocence. Pink is also connected to femininity, which is often thought of as nurturing, tender and compassionate.

Where To Use: It is a whimsical colour and it works well with grey, turquoise and muted orange. Pink is popular for children's bedrooms and playrooms to keep a sense of innocence, but it's best to avoid for family rooms and adult bedrooms. Mixing pink with dark wood, modern finishes and furniture can make a pink room look opulent.

Where Not To Use: Pastel pink has a calming effect in smaller doses, but if used too much can cause a restless feeling so be careful about overusing it in bedrooms, dining areas or offices.

MEANING
Love
Calm
Respect
Warmth
Delicate
Feminine
Intuition
Care
Assertive
Sensitive

PAINT FINISHES

& WHEN TO USE THEM

⟶

 **MATTE**

> Non-reflective appearance
> Hides imperfections
> Good for low-traffic areas, such as dining rooms, offices, ceilings

 **EGGSHELL**

> Velvety appearance
> Somewhat easy to clean
> Good for moderate-traffic areas, such as bedrooms and living rooms

 **SATIN**

> Slightly reflective appearance
> Easy to clean
> Good for moderate- to high-traffic areas, such as kitchens and bathrooms

 **GLOSS**

> Reflective surface
> Resistant to dirt and mildew
> Easy to clean
> Good for high-traffic areas and decorative statements, such as doors and trims

COLOUR
IN CONTEXT

Client: Burrow Holiday Park
Photographer: Philip Lauterbach

Theme: Oceanic Luxury
Project: Robswall by Hollybrook
Client: Hollybrook Homes
Agent: Knight Frank Ireland

SAVE YOUR *SWATCHES*

NAME:

BRAND:

NOTES:

NAME:

BRAND:

NOTES:

NAME:

BRAND:

NOTES:

NAME:

BRAND:

NOTES:

NAME:

BRAND:

NOTES:

NAME:

BRAND:

NOTES:

SAVE YOUR *SWATCHES*

NAME:

BRAND:

NOTES:

NAME:

BRAND:

NOTES:

NAME:

BRAND:

NOTES:

NAME:

BRAND:

NOTES:

NAME:

BRAND:

NOTES:

NAME:

BRAND:

NOTES:

5 ROOMS

99

*THE DESIGNER'S JOB IS
TO IMAGINE THE WORLD,
NOT HOW IT IS, BUT HOW
IT SHOULD BE.*

TERENCE CONRAN

THE LIVING ROOM

A living room, also called a lounge, sitting room or drawing room, is a room for relaxing and socialising in a residential house or apartment. This room was historically called a front room as it was traditionally near the main entrance at the front of the house, where the host would seat guests as they entered the house.

Theme: Modern Traditions
Project: Foxburrow
Client: Hollybrook Homes
Agents: Hume Auctioneers
Sponsor: DFS

WHAT ARE THE
TOP 10 TIPS?

AU NATUREL

Natural light should fill this space wherever possible, so elect for larger windows, glass doors and translucent partitions within doors. The daylight will change over the course of the day, which will change the perception of space at different times. Ensure harmony between natural and artificial light to strengthen the feeling of spaciousness in the room. Even a small room can make use of the maximum light available, which will also save on costs for artificial light.

ILLUMINATION

The choice of lighting plays an important role in the composition of the room. When the ceiling is low, indirect light such as floor and table lamps are useful. Otherwise, built-in lamps can be used so they do not steal attention. With high ceilings, low hanging lights over side tables make a lovely feature. Try to seek a balance between a sense of comfort and luminosity to highlight every detail.

ZONE RIGHT

As this is a multipurpose area for a variety of people, opt for at least two zones. A zone is an area within a room that has a specific purpose, such as living and lounging, watching TV, reading, relaxing alone or relaxing with others. The choice and arrangement of furniture is key to getting the different zones right. Lighting should complement each zone too.

THEME THE SCHEME

The most important living room décor is the furniture, which should stem from a core theme. To get started, let's check out my top ten themes: Scandinavian, Contemporary, Industrial, Country House, Rustic, Mediterranean, Modern, Asian, Vintage, Minimalist and Victorian Eccentric. Whatever theme you choose, this starting point is key to bringing the room to life.

BOLD OR BRIGHT

Opting for bold colours, especially on the walls and furniture, creates a statement. For darker bold colours, embrace their intensity in smaller rooms using green or navy throughout the space. Light neutrals can help the space feel larger and help induce feelings of calm, relaxation and comfort. Neutral colours can be combined with bold accessories.

CURTAINS

Curtains can be a beautiful addition to a living room. With a variety of colours, designs and textures available, the choice is virtually limitless. Curtains allow for privacy in public-facing rooms or can block out strong sunlight glare. Made-to-measure curtains are more expensive than made-to-measure blinds, and can often be one of the more costly additions to any interior space.

MIRROR MAGIC

Mirrors can help create a sense of breadth or depth in any space. Used strategically, they add value to a room in different ways. For example, a mirror can make the room look bigger. Cabinets with mirrored doors can make the space more versatile and bring more elegance to its composition. Mirrors can be used across the surface of an entire wall or just in a single area of detail, such as over a fireplace.

DÉCOR DIY

You could leave your walls free to channel all attention to one central art piece, or you could allow for the wall décor to become a style feature in itself. Mixing posters, art and photography can create great décor opportunities for a living room.

UPCYCLE & UPHOLSTERY

If you have a limited budget, consider re-upholstering your existing furniture. Mixing new investment pieces with upcycled furniture can bring a new lease of life to any space, and it is good for the environment.

SUSTAINABLE STYLING

Accessories are key to bringing your theme together, particularly for eclectic designer or minimalist styles, where considering how all the pieces will work together is crucial. When sources accessories, think about supporting local businesses or investing in sustainable designers. If your budget is already stretched, head to charity shops or vintage fairs, where you can find one-of-a-kind pieces that are budget and environmentally friendly.

Theme: City Chic
Project: 20 Hanover Riverside
Agent: Owen Reilly Estate Agents

Theme: Art Deco | Gatsby
Project: Robswall by Hollybrook
Client: Hollybrook Homes
Agent: Knight Frank Ireland
Photographer: Declan Cassidy

WHAT IS YOUR
SEATING STYLE?

1. Arm chair
2. Arm chair with foot stool
3. Chaise longe
4. Love seat
5. Two-seater sofa
6. Three-seater sofa
7. Corner sofa
8. L-shaped sofa

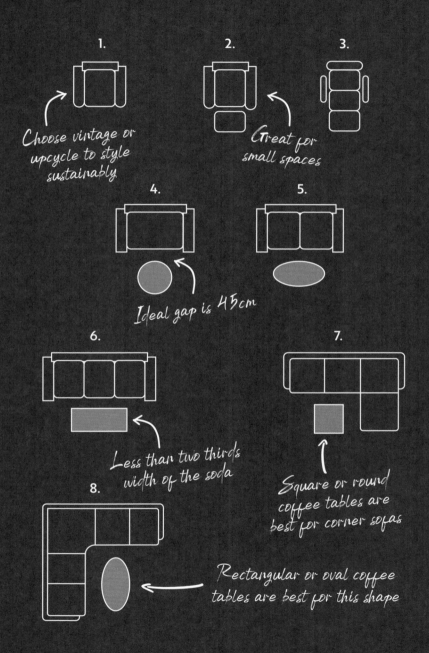

1.

Choose vintage or upcycle to style sustainably

2.

Great for small spaces

3.

4.

5.

Ideal gap is 45cm

6.

Less than two thirds width of the sofa

7.

Square or round coffee tables are best for corner sofas

8.

Rectangular or oval coffee tables are best for this shape

SAMPLE FLOOR PLAN

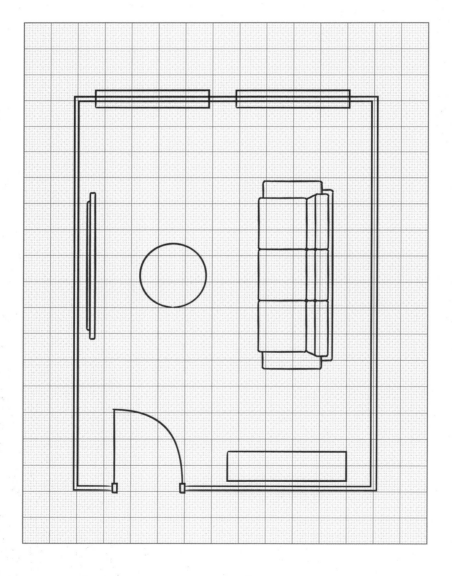

DESIGN TIME:
TIME FOR YOU TO CREATE YOUR OWN LIVING ROOM PLAN

YOUR LIVING ROOM **TO-DO LIST**

TASK	✓

YOUR LIVING ROOM **TO-DO LIST**

TASK	✓

THE DINING ROOM

A dining room is a room reserved primarily for eating meals – breakfast, lunch or dinner. While other activities may also take place there outside of meal times, it is known as the key entertaining space, so style and character are key. Nowadays, the dining room is usually adjacent to the kitchen for convenience in serving, although in the past, it was often on an entirely different floor level.

Theme: Oceanic Luxury
Project: Robswall by Hollybrook
Client: Hollybrook Homes
Agent: Knight Frank Ireland

WHAT ARE THE
TOP 10 TIPS?

FEATURE LIGHTING

Lighting over dining areas is fundamental and it offers a great opportunity to create a feature piece. There are many choices that can look great above a dining table, such as pendant lights, pendant suspension lights, non-linear multi-pendant light fixtures, multi-tiered pendants, modern chandeliers or even recessed lighting. Round tables look especially nice with modern chandeliers or rounded pendants, or even multi-tiered pendants. Floor and table lamps can be added around the room as a lower budget choice. However, less is more in this room because the key focus should be the dining area.

ADD & SUBTRACT

Subtract any furniture, accessories and art that no longer serve this space. Ensure you have the option to add extra seating and furniture for guests, even taking chairs from another room or buying an extendable dining table. Build a central theme with your choice of art, accessories and furniture to complement this space and reflect your character and style.

PAINT & PAPER

Invest in a re-paint of the entire space to transform it. Or, if your budget does not permit, paint key areas such as doors and window frames to emphasise key structural features. For smaller spaces, opt for neutral colours to ensure the space looks larger. For larger spaces, choose on-trend colours to highlight the space in interesting ways.

SUITABLY STYLE

Choose a theme suitable for all the different areas and users of the space. Research until you find a style you like. Use Pinterest, Instagram, and magazines to plan a suitable theme for this key area. Similar to the living room, the dining room is a central area for yourself, your family and friends to enjoy on a day-to-day and seasonal basis, so it should be styled with care.

TOP TABLE

For a complete transformation, invest in a statement table and chairs which can be the central focus of this space. Choosing your top table style, whether round, asymmetrical, square, rectangular or extendable, is key to ensuring it will be loved and used all year round. For this piece, in particular if the space is a small, you may want to consider investing in vintage.

ACCESSORY LIGHT

For final details, add scented candles, lamps and fireplaces if you have access. With Irish weather and winter approaching – always try to add as much light as you can to your home and life!

SUPPORT LOCAL

It is important more than ever to support local businesses, which will bolster the national economy while helping these small businesses remain open during difficult times. Whether it is online shops, boutiques or larger stores, there are so many options where you can source your art, tableware and other interiors choices.

DYNAMIC DRAWERS

The dining room is where you eat, but you can also store your glasses and tableware there. Investing in a stylish chest of drawers that is functional yet beautiful will allow for you to store lots of accessories, nicely hidden away, and it will also add valuable storage space in this area that is often overlooked.

FUNCTIONAL FLOORING

Flooring choices will depend on your styles and preferences, but think about functionality as well. Wood and tiles are the standard flooring choices for rooms where you will serve food and drink. They are also much more hard-wearing than carpet. However, for comfort, add a rug to your dining room, which can be replaced or swapped out for different interior styles throughout the year.

TABLESCAPING TOUCHES

Tablescaping – styling and decorating your table in preparation for a meal – is an extremely popular hobby these days, especially among those who enjoy entertaining at home. Dining is the most common way of bringing friends and loved ones together on special occasions, including birthdays, anniversaries, Christmas and other holidays. So, investing in several tablescaping options would be an ideal investment if you want to create various beautiful spaces all year round.

YOUR TABLESCAPING
GUIDE

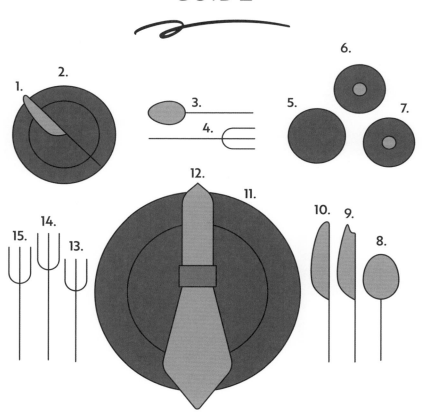

1. Butter knife
2. Bread plate
3. Dessert spoon
4. Dessert fork
5. Water glass
6. Red wine glass
7. White wine glass
8. Soup spoon
9. Fish knife
10. Dinner knife
11. Charger
12. Napkin
13. Salad fork
14. Dinner fork
15. Fish fork

FIND YOUR TABLESCAPE PLAN

Theme: Classic Contemporary
Project: Mount Stewart
Client: Hollybrook Homes
Agent: Hume Auctioneers
Photographer: Declan Cassidy

Theme: Oceanic Luxury
Project: Robswall by Hollybrook
Client: Hollybrook Homes
Agent: Knight Frank Ireland

Theme: Art Deco | Gatsby
Project: Robswall by Hollybrook
Client: Hollybrook Homes
Agent: Knight Frank Ireland
Photographer: Declan Cassidy

Theme: Modern Traditions
Project: Foxburrow
Client: Hollybrook Homes
Agents: Hume Auctioneers

WHAT IS YOUR
DINING STYLE?

6 SEATS

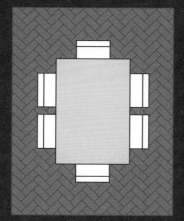

8 SEATS

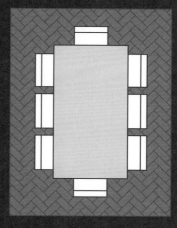

4 SEATS

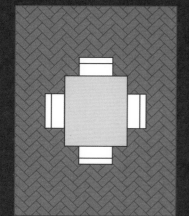

4 SEATS

SAMPLE FLOOR PLAN

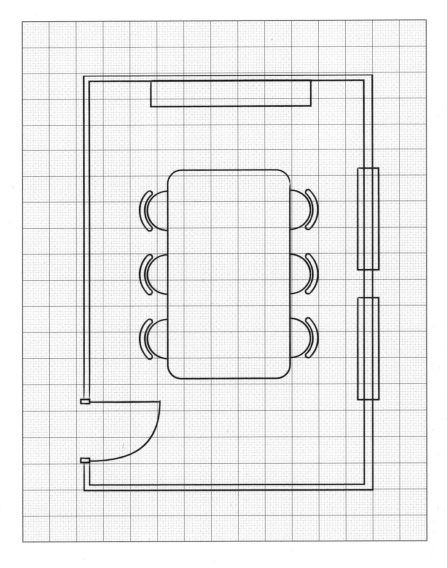

DESIGN TIME:
TIME FOR YOU TO CREATE YOUR OWN DINING ROOM PLAN

YOUR DINING ROOM **TO-DO LIST**

TASK	✓

YOUR DINING ROOM **TO-DO LIST**

TASK	✓

THE KITCHEN

A kitchen is the area used for the preparation and cooking of food. In modern homes, it is one of the most central areas, and is often designed as a kitchen-dining space.

Project: Robswall by Hollybrook
Client: Hollybrook Homes
Agent: Knight Frank Ireland
Photographer: Declan Cassidy

Project: Mount Stewart
Client: Hollybrook Homes
Agent: Hume Auctioneers
Photographer: Declan Cassidy

WHAT ARE THE
TOP 10 TIPS?

THE WORK TRIANGLE

This is a concept developed in the 1940s to maximise efficiency in the kitchen. The cooker, fridge, and sink should be close to one another, allowing for easy use of the kitchen. Try to plan your kitchen around this idea because it helps make it a more functional space. The work triangle is flexible and can be adapted to suit various kitchen shapes.

NEW OR RENEW?

Investing in a new kitchen is a pleasure and always worthwhile but it can become costly and time-consuming. For new homes, kitchens are generally included in the budget at the early stages. In an existing home, however, you could re-invent the kitchen by re-spraying it, which costs approximately 15–20% of an entirely new kitchen. If yours is a new-build or your budget allows it, work with a kitchen company or designer to ensure you get the best value kitchen that suits your requirements. You want to build a kitchen that will be long lasting.

SEATING STYLES

When designing a kitchen, opt for zones with the primary zone being the work triangle. Then add additional zones if space is available. If there is room, you could add a dining area, such as an island bar with stools or a dining table and chairs – whichever makes the best use of space, and suits your family's needs. A table seating area also offers options for working, studying, or watching TV when it is not being used for dining.

GARDEN VIEWPOINT

If you have access to a garden or balcony it is highly recommended to join your kitchen to this access point. The benefits include natural light, fresh air, removing bad odours and hosting outdoor dining. When purchasing new homes, look for those with garden access.

INTEGRATED OR FREESTANDING?

Depending on your style, you must decide whether you want integrated or freestanding machines and appliances. These include coffee machines, microwaves, and even dishwashers. Always consider buying sustainable products from local brands. Consider, too, the finish of the appliance. You want it to be durable and easy to clean. Think about working with a designer, kitchen company or appliance company to curate a bespoke style for your needs while supporting local.

ADDITIONAL AREAS

Include additional zones if feasible and work them into your plans and budgets. These zones could include, a storage area, pantry, utility room, pet area, desk area, library area or exercise area – all depending on the size of the space and your requirements.

STYLE CHIC

Choose a theme suitable for the various uses of the kitchen space, while keeping in mind the style of the rest of your home. Research online (Pinterest and Instagram) and in magazines to create a theme for this key area, ensuring the finishes and appliances are stylish functional and durable.

BLINDS BESPOKE

For practical purposes, blinds in kitchens, utility and wet areas are best in terms of function, and are better for the budget. Roman blinds are popular for kitchens and you can colour match your blinds with your colour scheme, or opt for neutral blinds. You can also combine blinds with curtains, to get the best of both styles.

SHELVES & STORAGE

Think about every task you might perform in the kitchen so you can best plan the space. For example, you want a smooth clean-up after meals, so think about how far the sink or dishwasher will be from the dining area. If you have a utility area, building integrated storage for coats, bags and shoes will help the area function as a mud room too. Also, don't forget about coat hooks – they are easy to install and highly functional.

FLOORING FRENZY

The kitchen flooring can be stylish and showstopping, but it must be hard-wearing and waterproof. Choose dark flooring for a contemporary look or marble for a more luxurious feel. Statement patterned tiles can be ideal on the floor or backsplash areas. Wood can be applied in different ways – a herringbone pattern is very on-trend, while dark wood is plush, and lighter wood can give a contemporary look. Underfloor heating or adding rugs are great for keeping cosy throughout the winter months.

Theme: Modern Traditions
Project: Foxburrow
Client: Hollybrook Homes
Agents: Hume Auctioneers

SAMPLE FLOOR PLAN

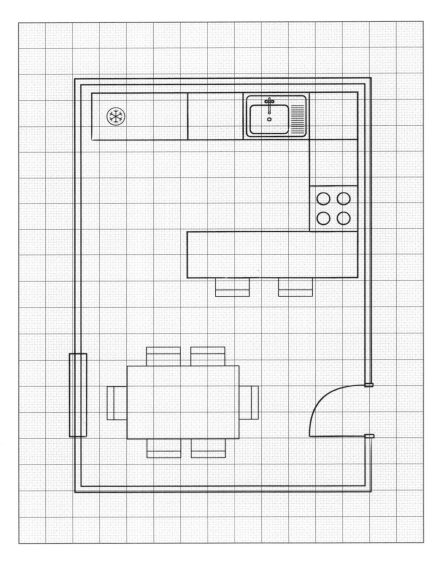

DESIGN TIME:
TIME FOR YOU TO CREATE YOUR OWN KITCHEN PLAN

YOUR KITCHEN **TO-DO LIST**

TASK	✓

YOUR KITCHEN **TO-DO LIST**

TASK	✓

THE BATHROOM

A bathroom is a room for personal hygiene, generally containing a bathtub or a shower. In the past, homes usually had separate bathrooms and toilets (or WCs – water closets), but nowadays, it is more common to have the toilet in the bathroom as well.

Project: Robswall by Hollybrook
Client: Hollybrook Homes
Agent: Knight Frank Ireland
Photographer: Declan Cassidy

Client: Burrow Holiday Park
Photographer: Declan Cassidy

WHAT ARE THE
TOP 10 TIPS?

WALLPAPER WANDERLUST

Installing wallpaper in any room ensures a dramatic impact. Patterned wallpaper is a current trend, and includes geometric patterns or natural-effect wallpaper, which are both wonderful ways to style any wet room. Just make sure you choose waterproof wallpaper. You can also find durable vinyl with marble textures, or even with metallic effects, which are also perfect for bathrooms. Place these behind a bathtub or shower as a feature wall to truly bring the space to life!

OUTDOORS INTERIORS

Outdoor indoors are key trends in the home, particularly for bathrooms. For instance, if you add a natural effect by applying wood or faux wood finishes, it can provide a calming contrast with tiles, basins and other shiny surfaces. In addition, wooden tiles (which imitate the look of wooden floors) and wooden furniture can bring a sense of the great outdoors into the bathroom.

FREESTANDING FANCY

Freestanding bathtubs are on trend and will remain so for a while. A tub can bring art deco styles to life, especially if it is paired with gold accents and striking floor tiles. Freestanding tubs can also be used in a modern way if the bathroom is finished with a Carrara marble look, for example. For added impact, invest in a block-colour bath, such as grey matched against dark stone, which will create a sleek and stylish wet room.

TILING TOUCHES

Tiling is commonly used in bathrooms and the choices are abundant. Decide on a style, size and colour ensure you keep to two or three choices, or mix them with patterned tiles. Make sure they suit your budget, style, and are durable for long-term wear.

MIX & MATCH

Mix and match materials to ensure you create your own style. Particularly if you have gone for an eclectic style where you mix modern and vintage pieces around your home. If you prefer a modern style, then mix and match tiles in block colours, or choose different finishes and materials. Also, add textures to build up layers and add depth to the space.

SMOOTH STATEMENTS

With our lives busier than ever before, many people think of their bathroom as a relaxing space. Soothing, serene, smooth surfaces and organic materials are popular for bathrooms. For these effects, look at using large tiles or monochromatic stone, matte black fixtures, and oak-wood surfaces. Alternatively, choosing unusual colours such as green, navy or coral can be powerful in these spaces because they are unexpected.

ITALIAN STYLE

Italian style is a timeless trend and uses tiles as the central focus. Carrara marble is popular as a luxurious tile, while mosaic tiles add the perfect finish to create an indulgent space. Key colours are white, grey, navy, green, or multicolour. Combine with brushed gold, brushed chrome or silver accessories to bring this timeless style to life!

COMPACT CHIC

Less is more – and not just in minimalist décor. So, it is worth observing the advantages of using 'furniture to measure'. Compact household appliances are always very welcome in apartments and smaller homes. They bring flexibility to the rooms and allow for the best use of each space. Examples include creating wall-to-ceiling units or integrated bathroom units, showers and baths.

BESPOKE BLINDS

Blinds come in a variety of colours and are easy to wash and keep clean, which is ideal for wet rooms. Many are also resistant to mould. There are a variety of choices, such as roller blinds, which allow lots of light in, or vertical and venetian blinds, which give more privacy. Day and night blinds are a cheaper alternative to electric blinds, which are ideal for adding a modern touch.

ACCENT ACCESSORIES

Invest in accent accessories such a mirrors, towels, robes and bathmats to colour match your scheme. For a serene style, opt for all white, which will give a hotel-like finish. Use simplistic styles on frames and mirrors. Diffusers, candles and indoor plants are perfect accessories to help you enjoy this space.

Theme: Giorno e Notte
Project: Robswall by Hollybrook
Client: Hollybrook Homes
Agent: Knight Frank Ireland
Photographer: Declan Cassidy

Photographer: Barry McCall
Credit: Rocca Stone & Marble

SAMPLE FLOOR PLAN

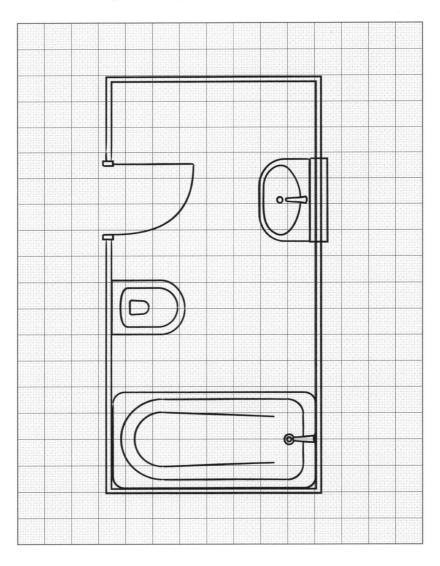

DESIGN TIME:
TIME FOR YOU TO CREATE YOUR OWN BATHROOM PLAN

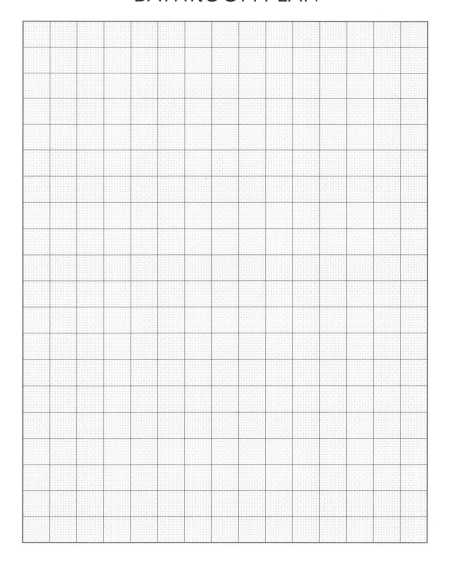

YOUR BATHROOM **TO-DO LIST**

TASK	✓

YOUR BATHROOM **TO-DO LIST**

TASK	✓

THE HALLWAY

The hallway is the space that leads in from the front entrance of a home. It often goes all the way along to the back entrance, and leads to other rooms. There are also hallways on each floor of a house, which are also known as landings. They lead from the stairs to the upstairs rooms. The front hall is the first space in your home that visitors will see, and how it looks is key to welcoming family and guests with the best impression.

Project: Robswall by Hollybrook
Client: Hollybrook Homes
Agent: Knight Frank Ireland
Photographer: Declan Cassidy

Project: Mount Stewart
Client: Hollybrook Homes
Agent: Hume Auctioneers
Photographer: Declan Cassidy

Project: Robswall by Hollybrook
Client: Hollybrook Homes
Agent: Knight Frank Ireland
Photographer: Declan Cassidy

WHAT ARE THE
TOP 10 TIPS?

CLEAN & CLEAR

Clear all unused furniture and accessories from the floors and walls to keep your hallway uncluttered. Have just a side table or morros to ensure there is plenty of space for visitors to move through this key space.

LIGHT VERSUS DARK

Choose your side – dark or white. Add wallpaper, paneling or paint to bring the space to life. You could create a moody space with dark, bold colours and dramatic lighting. Or you can play it safe with grey. Either way, choose a statement style.

FRAME TIME

Make key walls in the hallways stand out by displaying art, mirrors, photography or books on them. Display items individually, in threes or in a grid style for the most impact.

FEATURED FLOORING

Tiles are a great choice for the hallway because they are practical in terms of maintenance, and they can make a big a statement depending on the style you choose. Wooden floors can also add style – try a herringbone pattern or mixed-width planks to make a great first impression.

LIBRARY WALL ART

Hang art on a feature wall using different frames, or a mix of artists and styles. For the best visuals, hang in groups of threes. This works well in hallways and along the stairs, and it's a great way for art collectors to display their favourites.

ART AND LIGHT

Combining beautiful art and interesting lighting features can be a very effective way to highlight your art and create a big impact in your hallway or landing space.

MIRROR WALLS

Mirrors are an ideal solution for a smaller space. A mirror reflects the light and visually opens up the area – which helps make the most of smaller hallways. Mirrors are also very effective when placed opposite or near art and photography.

STAIRCASE CHIC

Hallways are fundamental spaces for transitioning from one room to another. Consider investing in a statement or wrap-around staircase to both fill the space and add a feature piece. Adding mouldings, panelling and statement lighting can truly bring the hallways and stairways to life!

STATEMENT ART

Select one piece of art to create a statement piece in your hallway. Choose a piece by your favourite artist or photographer, or a favourite family portrait.

LIGHT IT UP

Lighting in this space is of paramount importance. Open any adjoining windows to allow in natural light. Work to create layers in lighting which will brighten the space without being overbearing or costly. Mirrors in hallways and small areas reflect light, making it brighter. There are many types of lighting – don't forget about candles or lamps. Let light in!

Client: Burrow Holiday Park
Photographer: Declan Cassidy

GALLERY WALL
PLACEMENT
IDEAS

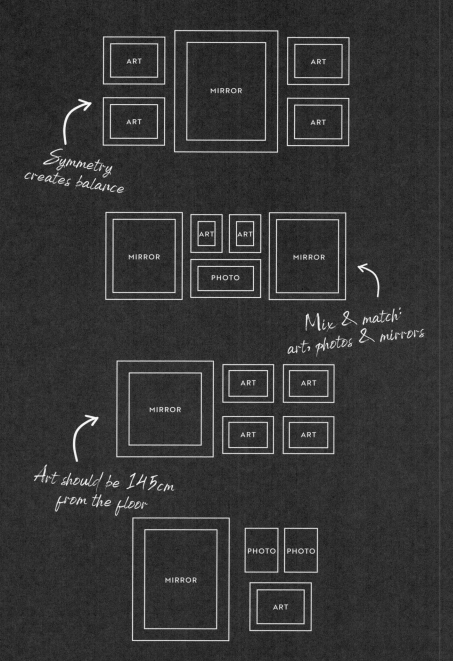

Symmetry creates balance

Mix & match: art, photos & mirrors

Art should be 145cm from the floor

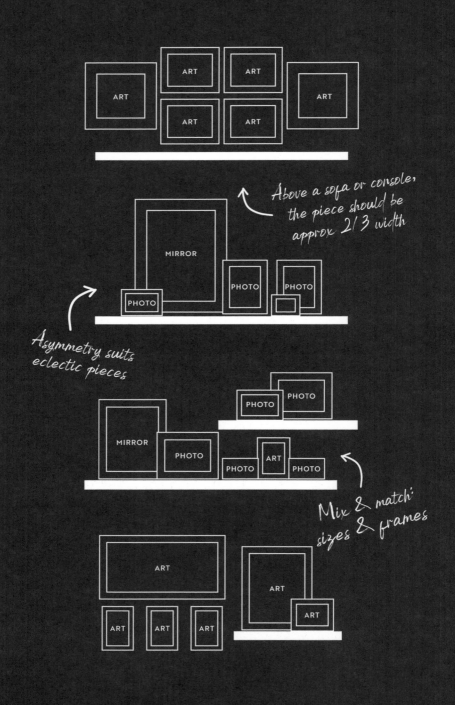

ART

ART ART

ART ART

ART

MIRROR

PHOTO

PHOTO PHOTO

Above a sofa or console, the piece should be approx 2/3 width

Asymmetry suits eclectic pieces

PHOTO PHOTO

MIRROR PHOTO

PHOTO ART PHOTO

Mix & match sizes & frames

ART

ART ART ART

ART ART

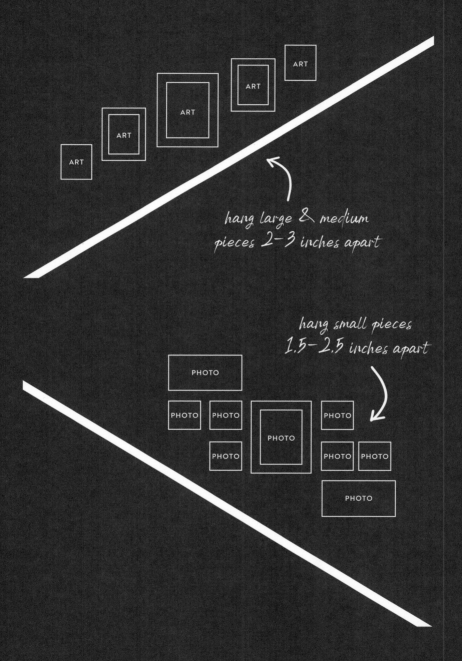

hang large & medium
pieces 2–3 inches apart

hang small pieces
1.5–2.5 inches apart

SAMPLE FLOOR PLAN

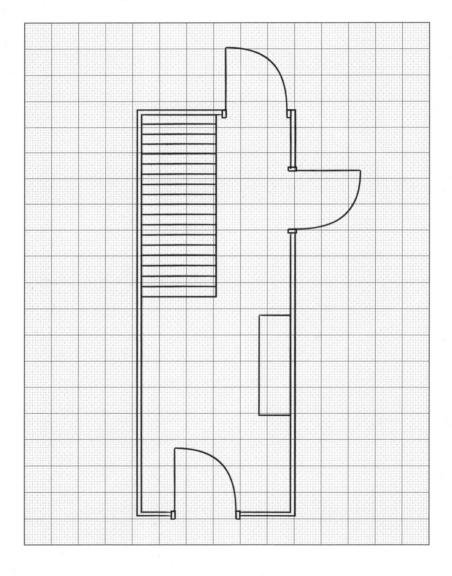

DESIGN TIME:
TIME FOR YOU TO CREATE YOUR OWN HALLWAY PLAN

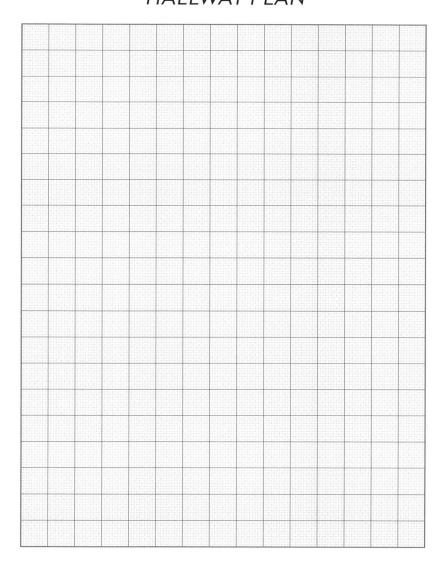

YOUR HALLWAY **TO-DO LIST**

TASK	✓

YOUR HALLWAY **TO-DO LIST**

TASK	✓

THE OFFICE

A home office is an area in a person's residence reserved for business activities. Nowadays, a home office often serves as a multipurpose area for work, study, exercise or even as a playroom. It can also be a shared space within a different room such as a spare room, main bedroom or attic so that it can be used when required.

Theme: Giorno e Notte
Project: Robswall by Hollybrook
Client: Hollybrook Homes
Agent: Knight Frank Ireland
Photographer: Declan Cassidy

Theme: Oceanic Luxury
Project: Robswall by Hollybrook
Client: Hollybrook Homes
Agent: Knight Frank Ireland

WHAT ARE THE
TOP 10 TIPS?

CREATE SPACE

Choose an optimum place within the property for the office. If there is a spare room, that makes the most sense. However, if there are no spare rooms available, choose a space that will enable you to separate your working and personal areas, for example a corner of the dining room. If, from the office area, you can see laundry, kids' toys or distractions such as the TV or phone, it is easy to get side-tracked when you should be working. Finding a space that is separate will help you get the most out of your office.

FURNITURE ZONES

Try to keep a distinction between work and relaxation areas. If you designate a spare bedroom as the office, try to keep the bed and desk in separate parts of the room. If there is not enough space for different areas, then opt for a foldable desk and chair, which can be easily stowed under the bed or in a closet to ensure you can set up a working area when needed. Use the walls to designate the office area of a room with feature walls using paint, wallpaper and art.

STORAGE SOLUTIONS

Plan ahead so you have the appropriate solutions required. Choose stylish shelving and bookcase units that can serve as a feature wall as well as holding books and ornaments. While decorating this room, invest in dynamic drawers to allow for extra space for filing, books and receipts.

LIGHT & SOUND

Ensuring you have adequate lighting for your work environment is key, and it may require some investment. If it's a new build, make sure the lighting plan includes enough lighting for the office area. Otherwise, add floor or table lamps to an existing space. Ideally combine with natural light.

SOUNDPROOF YOUR SPACE

Your work environment should be both relaxing and professional. Use soft furnishings to help reduce background noise during work calls and to protect your privacy.

DESK AREA

Why not invest in a DIY desk? It's very efficient to add a desk inside an alcove area or a walk-in closet as it uses space that is otherwise wasted. Face your desk away from the TV, bed, or kitchen area –towards a wall or window – to remove distraction. If you've only got a small bedroom to work with, try swapping out your nightstand for a desk.

MULTI-PURPOSE PURPOSES

Multi-use environments are a great selling point in any real estate project, as they really make the most of the space. For instance, being able to convert an office into a playroom is very useful, and can be done easily with the adjustable units and moveable furniture. Being able to transform a yoga area or gym space into an entertainment room can be achieved with a few storage units and maybe a mobile bar cart that can be brought in for social occasions. You could build a pet area in the base of a bookshelf, making the bookshelf dual-purpose. The options are endless, depending on your style, budget and household's requirements.

STYLISH SHELVING

Choose stylish shelving and bookcase units to create a feature wall that holds books, plants and ornaments. This is ideal for home offices, multipurpose rooms and bedrooms. Add positive and uplifting artworks to keep you motivated.

SCREEN STYLING

Using a curtain or screen is another effective way of separating work and sleep areas. This can be achieved with wooden screens, a curtain or a bespoke built-in screen across certain areas of the room, for example an alcove beside a desk. Opening and closing the curtain or screen will help signify the beginning or end of the workday, helping to ensure a work-life balance.

SCENTING

Adding plants, flowers or diffusers can bring an earthy, natural sense to your space. Choosing scented candles – such as La Bougie: The Secret Garden, my own scent – will help keep you centred and relaxed throughout the day.

Theme: City Chic
Project: 20 Hanover Riverside
Agent: Owen Reilly Estate Agents

Theme: Oceanic Luxury
Project: Robswall by Hollybrook
Client: Hollybrook Homes
Agent: Knight Frank Ireland

SAMPLE FLOOR PLAN

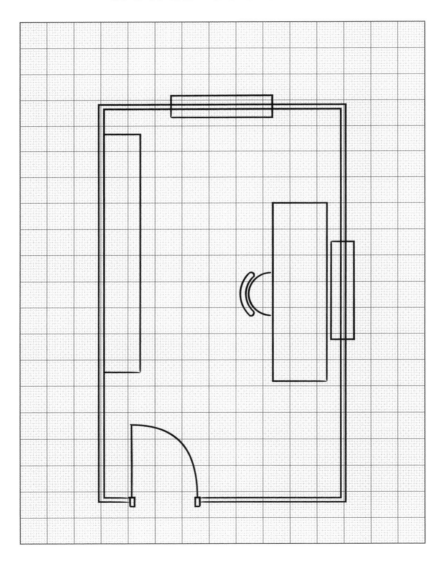

DESIGN TIME:
TIME FOR YOU TO CREATE YOUR OWN OFFICE PLAN

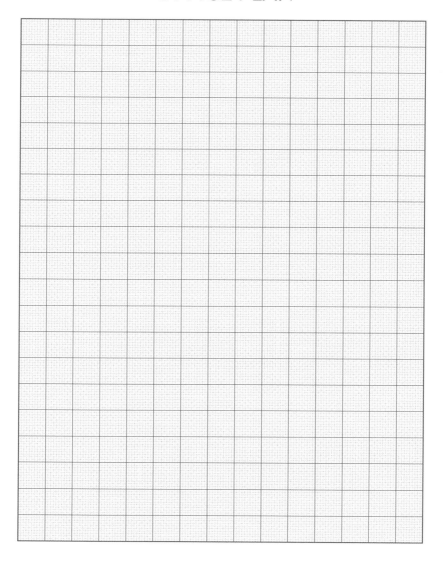

YOUR OFFICE **TO-DO LIST**

TASK	✓

YOUR OFFICE **TO-DO LIST**

TASK	✓

THE BEDROOM

The bedroom serves many functions and, now more than ever, a bedroom has taken on a more multipurpose role. First and foremost, a bedroom is a place to sleep. But it is also a place to study, entertain friends, watch TV and relax. The key here is how to combine these vastly different uses into one space and to ensure it remains a suitable room for sleeping and switching off.

Theme: Giorno e Notte
Project: Robswall by Hollybrook
Client: Hollybrook Homes
Agent: Knight Frank Ireland
Photographer: Declan Cassidy

WHAT ARE THE
TOP 10 TIPS?

COLOUR SCHEME

Traditionally, it was common practice to choose a bold colour scheme for the bedroom, such green or navy. There was also the convention to use more neutral colours, such as cream, beige or grey. Nowadays, going beyond convention is the best way to design a bedroom. Choose colours that suit your style and personal preference. For smaller spaces, choose all white or go bold with a darker blue or other striking colour of your choice. For larger spaces, chose a colour to match the lighting levels; for darker rooms with less light go bright and for well-lit rooms choose darker colours.

CURTAINS OR BLINDS

Choose curtains or blinds that are neutral or easily adaptable in case you later decide to change the styling of the bedroom. When choosing curtains versus blinds in your bedroom it comes down to personal preference. Whichever you choose, try to include a blackout function as this will help you sleep better. Blinds are a simpler option and are quite functional rather than beautiful, while curtains offer more options and can give a more luxurious look, particularly with carpets in the room.

SMART STORAGE

To create maximum space within your home, invest in storage solutions. You can add storage over the bed, under the bed, and even within the bed (as with an ottoman bed). The best bedroom storage solutions are those that are functional but which can be easily hidden. Open wardrobes are a stylish option that can add a decorative feature to the room with the colours of clothes mixed with books, art, storage boxes, etc. More importantly, they give the maximum space for storing clothes, shoes, handbags and so on.

CLOSET COMPACT

Invest in compact closets for your bedroom or commercial space. Choose one unified colour to help make the space look bigger while keeping the room stylish. If there is space for a closet, create different sections for each person to give it a functional structure and ensure it serves its organisational purpose.

SHOE STORAGE

Invest in storage boxes for shoes, bags or other accessories. These are both stylish and functional in any room. They can be placed into a wardrobe unit or stacked up to keep things organised, even in small spaces.

CLASSIC CHOICES

Choose an ottoman that allows storage while offering a place to sit or on which to place objects. This will keep the room stylish and chic. Depending on the style of the room, you might want to add some classic chests of drawers from a local market or vintage furniture store. They are practical for storage and also work as home décor.

BED BESPOKE

The choice of bed is perhaps most important when designing a bedroom. Choose a style that matches your colour scheme and make sure the measurements work in your space. When choosing a bed for a room that will be a home office as well, think about whether you need a bed that can move or transform in some way to keep the room layout flexible. For instance, an office with a sofa bed will allow the room to function year-round as a home office. A modern bunk bed with a desk underneath is another stylish idea that maximises floor space.

FLOOR FINISHES

Invest in rugs over durable wooden flooring, which can be cleaned or replaced when necessary. They also help reduce noise in the room. If you opt for carpets, choose darker colours, which tend to last longer and don't show as much dirt over time.

DRAWER-FOR-YOU

Large bookcases and utility units are obvious choices in which to store your ornaments and other objects, but they take up a lot of space. There are, however, often overlooked areas that could be extremely useful. Small drawers can be attached to the side of the headboard to store bedside objects, such as glasses or books. Bedside units or slimline desks with drawers can hold personal, children's or pet accessories while maximising the space.

ART & ACCESSORIES

Combining art, mirrors, photography and decorative accessories will enhance the bedroom space and invite you in with a welcoming glow. If you think this will be too distracting, then keep the space minimal to ensure it is a place of serenity where you can relax and unwind.

Theme: Modern Traditions
Project: Foxburrow
Client: Hollybrook Homes
Agents: Hume Auctioneers

Client: Burrow Holiday Park
Photographer: Declan Cassidy

SAMPLE FLOOR PLAN

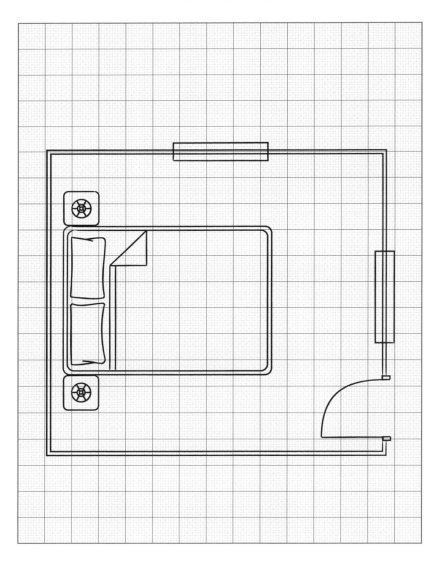

DESIGN TIME:
TIME FOR YOU TO CREATE YOUR OWN BEDROOM PLAN

YOUR BEDROOM **TO-DO LIST**

TASK	✓

YOUR BEDROOM **TO-DO LIST**

TASK	✓

CHILDREN'S BEDROOMS

A children's bedroom, baby's room or nursery is used primarily for sleeping, though many children will store their toys in their rooms and play there too. Nowadays, it has become common to create a theme for young children's bedrooms that can be easily transitioned into an older child's room as they move into their teens.

Credit: iStock

Client: Burrow Holiday Park
Photographer: Declan Cassidy

WHAT ARE THE
TOP 10 TIPS?

SURVEY THE SPACE

Review your space and to keep to a budget. Decide the key areas in which you will design your theme. For example, if there is a unique feature, such as an alcove or bay window, then dress up the space. This helps you prioritise which area to focus on.

RE-COLOUR

Create a colour scheme. For neutral, use either all white or white enhanced with greys. If your home already has bold colours, use a darker colour to fit in with the rest of the house. Then you can add two or three accent colours to the key areas to give the room its own personality. Use Christmas spray paint in white and gold tree to add touches of sparkle throughout.

LIGHT-IT-UP

Create layers in lighting to ensure the child will have a bright, airy room. Think about where to place lamps or night lights in the space that will work with your child's needs.

SIMPLY STYLE

Add accent furniture or art with your child's favourite colours. Add interest to the room with rugs, bedding, throws, and curtains. All-white or neutral rooms in particular will require extra textures and accents.

BLINDS OR CURTAINS?

A child's room can have a playful design, so why not go for an unconventional style with your choice of blinds or curtains. Patterns or pictures on the blinds or curtains can tie in with the theme of the room and bring everything to life.

MULTIFUNCTIONAL FUNCTIONS

Your best bet is to choose multifunctional furniture for a child's room. Find a bed with under-bed storage, bunk beds or cabin beds with a desk underneath. Avoid over-cluttering to allow for a play area, and consider whether there is space for a larger bed, desk or workspace for when your child is older. Choose sustainable modular furniture, (TIPTOE's) such as a desk with modular legs and frames that can be adapted as your child grows, while teaching them about sustainability.

WALL-ART-CHIC

Frames, in particular gallery walls, are a perfect way to add an accent to a baby's bedroom. Hang up your preferred frames, prints and art, and add photos of your child as they grow up to create an evolving, personal display.

WALLPAPER WISH

Who said wallpaper was just for adults' rooms? Dress your child's walls with wall art or stickers, which can be a beautiful and simple way to decorate it. Alternatively, invest in neutral wallpaper as an inspirational feature.

CREATIVE CORNERS

Include a 'creative corner', which, depending on their age, can include a desk, playroom area, sports area, drawing wall or blackboard. This creates a distinct space where your child can relax and retreat while creating or playing.

PERSONALISED PERFECTION

Choose exactly which features to accentuate to make the room truly personalised to your child and your own style. For instance, decorate the ceiling with a beautiful pendant.

Credit: iStock

Client: Burrow Holiday Park
Photographer: Declan Cassidy

SAMPLE FLOOR PLAN

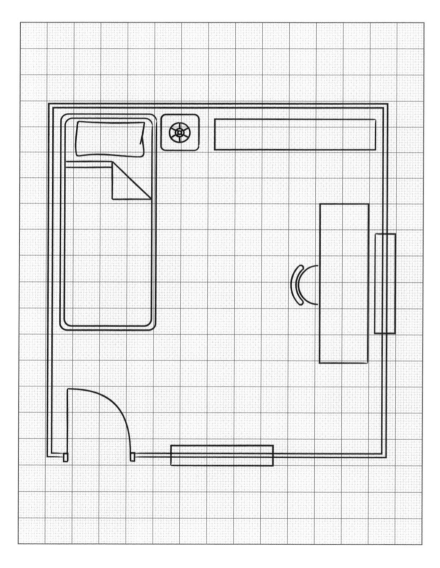

DESIGN TIME:
TIME FOR YOU TO CREATE YOUR OWN CHILDEN'S BEDROOM PLAN

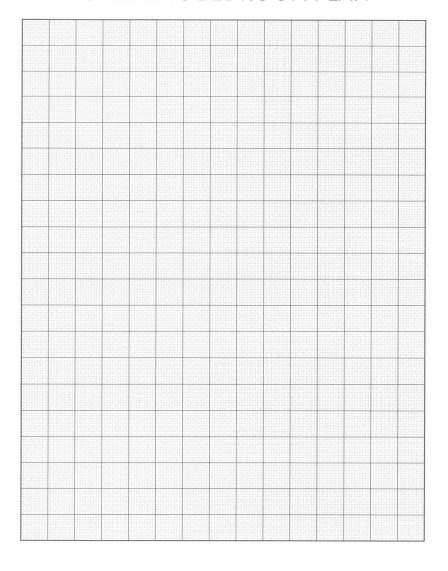

YOUR CHILDREN'S BEDROOM TO-DO LIST

TASK	✓

YOUR CHILDREN'S BEDROOM TO-DO LIST

TASK	✓

PET INTERIORS

A pet area will vary depending on your pet. For dogs, cats and other roaming pets, think about a multipurpose area where they can eat, sleep, play, wash and have their treats. Often, the pet area is set up in a utility room, kitchen or hallway area.

Credit: DFS

Credit: iStock

WHAT ARE THE
TOP 10 TIPS?

PET PERSONALISATION

Your pet area should be designed in accordance with your pet's size and needs, your personal needs, the available space and also your budget. You can buy a standard pet bed or cage that will fit your space. Or you can design a pet bed to fit in with one room's style, or you can install play areas right along an entire wall. Alternatively, you can add built-in aquariums or cages. There are unlimited options available online and in-store, so research right to get inspiration and create designs that work for your pet and your home alike.

STYLE SUSTAINABLY

With sustainability at the forefront of our design ethos, it is important tip to think about sustainability even for pet interiors. For instance, there are global and Irish brands that create bedding, accessories and pet collars that are eco-friendly. Small choices like this support both local business and help the environment.

DYNAMIC BEDS

Pet beds are important for the happiness and health of the pet. Cats and dogs spend a lot of time in their beds, which can be bulky. So you should try to find a suitable space to keep it. In smaller homes and homes with no garden, this can be more of an issue. There are plenty of creative ways to incorporate pet needs into a small space, such as housing beds or cages inside ventilated cabinets, on the bottom shelf of a bookcase, or in a small alcove. These creative solutions can work for all kinds of pet homes, including beds, cages for training and outdoor kennels and living areas.

CAT CLIMBING

Cats have a variety of needs that differ to those of dogs and other pets. Give your cat the chance to climb and move around – and don't forget the ability to go outside through a cat flap. Designing for a cat will include climbing spaces, scratching posts and a sleeping area. Various brands create chic and custom styles for this.

BIRDCAGE BESPOKE

For birds, there is a huge range of options for bird cages, which can be made into a beautiful feature in your living space. Choose a style that fits in with the rest of your home.

THINK TANK

For fish, turtles or snakes, tanks can be designed to suit your space. You can make them exciting by adding LED lights ornaments and rocks, which can be found in a store or from the local beach or nature area nearby. For rabbits or hamsters, invest in a stylish and sustainable hutch or cage, which will look nice in your home.

TREATS & TINS

Treats are part and parcel with having a pet. Store these in their own personalised tins to keep things organised while retaining a consistent pet theme throughout your home.

PET-FRIENDLY STORAGE

It is necessary to create maximum space within your home and investing in storage solutions for your pet needs are key. Designate a place near their bed or cage to store their other items. Buy a specific storage box or unit just for this purpose, or hide storage inside a cabinet or chest of drawers nearby.

CUSTOM CHIC

As with all interior design, it is ideal to install furniture that is made to measure for your pet. Compact beds and bespoke cages will be the best way to fit the pet's items seamlessly into your home. Custom items make the most of your space and can add flexible options to your rooms if necessary. Consider where you want to place the pet's living space and create custom furniture that will take into account your space, your style and your pet's needs, health and hygiene.

MATCHING MAGIC

A pet is for life so why not design your pet's space to match your own style? Paint or wallpaper beside their cage, tank or bed to create a unique space. Accessories with personal tags, especially if they match with children's rooms, are a great way to embrace the magic of pets in our lives!

Credit: iStock

Credit: iStock

YOUR PET INTERIORS **TO-DO LIST**

TASK	✓

YOUR PET INTERIORS **TO-DO LIST**

TASK	✓

OUTDOOR SPACES

Outdoor spaces include gardens, balconies, patios, terraces, verandas, courtyards or decking. All of these can be designed and styled in various ways. If you make your outdoor space welcoming, it will become an extension of your home.

Project: 20 Hanover Riverside
Agent: Owen Reilly Estate Agents

Project: RTE - *Find Me A Home*
Agent: Owen Reilly Estate Agents

WHAT ARE THE
TOP 10 TIPS?

EMBRACE YOUR SPACE

Whether you have a small balcony or a large garden, maximise what you have and try to include fundamental features such as seating (perhaps with an umbrella) and lighting. It's nice to add some decorative pieces such as luxury candles. For larger spaces, scale up. For smaller spaces, scale down. Either way, make sure you embrace the space.

AL FRESCO AMBIENCE

Despite the unpredictable weather, embrace a Mediterranean lifestyle by investing in beautiful seating with moveable colourful cushions to allow for a holiday ambience at home. Purchase some stylish blankets for late night outdoor dining too.

COOKING CHIC

Your outdoor space is the perfect environment for entertaining family and friends. To make the most of it, purchase a permanent or disposable barbeque and outdoor tableware sets to make cooking chic. Most importantly, create a space where people can spend quality time together.

GREEN & FAUX GRASS

For those who live in an apartment, having real grass may not be an option. So, invest in artificial grass which can provide a 'garden' feel on your balcony. For homes with gardens, artificial grass may be useful in areas that are difficult to maintain. Nonetheless, try to ensure that you include elements of natural grass or planting within your outdoor space to keep it green.

GARDEN RETREAT

Mobile wooden garden canopy areas are a growing trend. They are cost-effective and useful in both wet and extremely hot conditions, so they can be enjoyed by family and friends year-round.

PLANTING PLACEMENTS

Whether you have a natural passion for gardening or just enjoy the beautiful results, create space for plants and flowers at home. For smaller spaces, even a cactus or smaller plants with pops of colour will be a beautiful addition to any outdoor area.

STORAGE SOLUTIONS

Try to create maximum storage in your garden or patio without detracting from the space. Choose furniture with hidden storage or slimline sheds to store your garden items all year round.

COLOUR CONTRAST

Colours for outdoor furniture are on trend so choose statement colours such as pastel pink, green or mustard. Patterns are very popular too. The contrast of these colours against other outdoor furniture of natural woods and dark colours will help keep your outdoor space interesting. Dark colours for outdoor furniture remain popular as well, and can be combined with colourful accessories.

ECO LIGHTING

Choose stylish outdoor lighting to add some exciting features to your garden. At night, lights can fully transform a space. Choose LED or solar-powered lights, which are much better for the environment, and for your wallet.

OUTDOOR ACCESSORIES

In addition to furniture, invest in stylish and functional garden cushions, accessories and hanging plants. If gardening is your thing, have a set of tools, gloves and accessories and make sure you designate a place to store them.

Project: 20 Hanover Riverside
Agent: Owen Reilly Estate Agents

Project: Robswall by Hollybrook
Client: Hollybrook Homes
Agent: Knight Frank Ireland
Photographer: Declan Cassidy

SAMPLE FLOOR PLAN

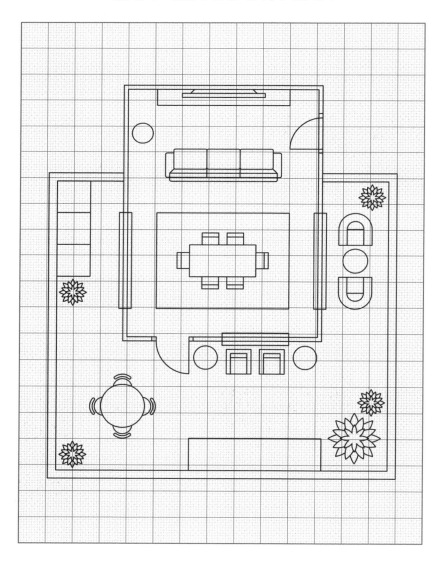

DESIGN TIME:
TIME FOR YOU TO CREATE YOUR OWN OUTDOOR SPACE FLOOR PLAN

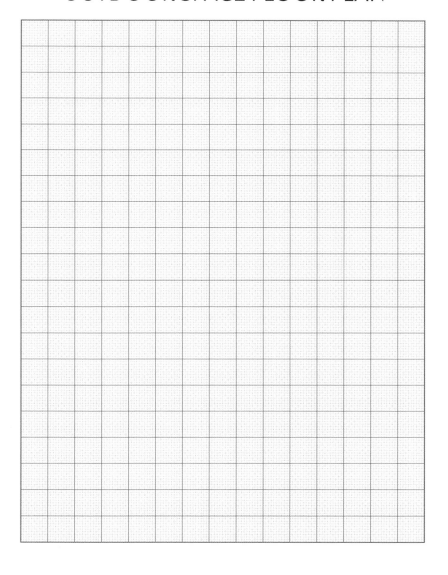

YOUR OUTDOOR SPACE **TO-DO LIST**

TASK	✓

YOUR OUTDOOR SPACE **TO-DO LIST**

TASK	✓

NOTES

"

*YOU HAVE TO KNOW WHAT
SPARKS THE LIGHT IN YOU SO
THAT YOU, IN YOUR OWN WAY,
CAN ILLUMINATE THE WORLD.*

OPRAH WINFREY

YOUR **NOTES**

YOUR **NOTES**

YOUR **NOTES**

YOUR **NOTES**

YOUR **NOTES**

YOUR **NOTES**

YOUR **NOTES**

YOUR NOTES

YOUR **NOTES**

YOUR **NOTES**

YOUR **NOTES**

YOUR **NOTES**

YOUR NOTES

YOUR **NOTES**

YOUR **NOTES**

YOUR NOTES

ABOUT
THE AUTHOR

Natasha Rocca Devine is an award-winning interior designer and author. Natasha created The Interiors NRD Studio to offer interior design and project management services, direct to residential and commercial clients in Ireland and internationally online. Natasha's work incorporates sustainability, eco design and Irish design as core features.

Natasha comes from a family of entrepreneurs and has been inspired from a young age by property and design, particularly from her family business, Rocca Tiles, which was created by her grandfather, Patrick. Natasha gained her first Masters in Journalism and Media Communications at Griffith College, Dublin, followed by a second in Interior Design and Architecture at KLC School of Design, London.

Since opening in 2018, The Interiors NRD Studio has received more than 23 awards for a portfolio of projects. Her clients include Knight Frank and Hollybrook Homes. Natasha's work has appeared on RTE One's *Find Me A Home*.

Natasha has also created two limited-edition sustainable candles with Irish candlemakers La Bougie, and she has written extensively on interior design for publications such as *The Sunday Business Post, The Sunday Independent* and *The Times*, while also sharing her expertise online.

theinteriorsnrd.com

SO, WE HAVE REACHED THE END... YET, IT IS ONLY THE BEGINNING.

IT WAS A PLEASURE TO BRING OUT THE INTERIOR DESIGNER IN YOU! I HOPE I HAVE HELPED YOU TO CREATE YOUR DREAM INTERIOR DESIGN PROJECT AND SAVED YOU TIME, STRESS AND MONEY ALONG THE WAY.

WISHING YOU THE VERY BEST IN YOUR NEW, IMPROVED HOME, RENTAL OR SALES PROPERTY. I CAN'T WAIT TO SEE YOUR END RESULT.

LOTS OF LIGHT,

Natasha xxx